More than Muscle:

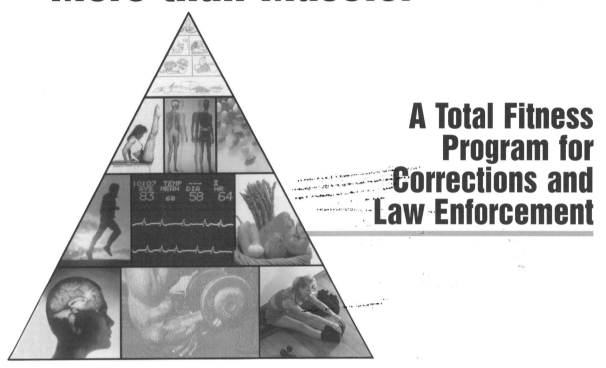

A Total Fitness Program for Corrections and Law Enforcement

The Variable Cyclic Phase System

American Correctional Association Staff

Betty Adams Green, President
James A. Gondles, Jr., CAE, Executive Director
Gabriella M. Daley, Director, Communications and Publications
Alice Fins, Publications Managing Editor
Michael Kelly, Associate Editor
Harry Wilhelm, Marketing Manager
Anne Hasselbrack, Editorial Assistant
Linnette Cunningham, Administrative Assistant

Cover design by Mike Selby, Graphics and Production Associate
Production by Capital Communications, Inc., Crofton, Maryland
Photography by Jerome Bird, Avis Media Services

Copyright 2000 by the American Correctional Association. All rights reserved. The reproduction, distribution, or inclusion in other publications of materials in this book is prohibited without prior written permission from the American Correctional Association. No part of this book may be reproduced by any electronic means including information storage and retrieval systems without permission in writing from the publisher.

Printed in the United States of America by Kirby Lithographic Company, Inc., Arlington, VA
ISBN 156991-118-5

This publication may be ordered from:
American Correctional Association
4380 Forbes Boulevard
Lanham, Maryland 20706-4322
1-800-222-5646
For information on publications and videos available from ACA, contact our worldwide web home page at: http://www.corrections.com/aca.

Library of Congress Cataloging-in-Publication Data
American Correctional Association
    More than muscle: a fitness program for corrections and law enforcement, the variable cyclic phase system/American Correctional Association.
        p. cm.
    Includes index.
    ISBN 1-56991-118-5 (pbk.)
    1. Police–Health and hygiene. 2. Correctional personnel–Health and hygiene. 3. Physical fitness. 4. Health promotion. 5. Stress management. I. Title.
    HV7936.H4 P43 2000
    99-088643

More than Muscle is based on a manuscript originally submitted to ACA by Jerry Pearson, formerly a physical fitness instructor and personal trainer for the Southern Colorado Law Enforcement Training Academy and professor of criminal justice at Trinidad Junior College. Since submission, it has been substantially revised and edited by the American Correctional Association staff and freelancer, Howard Kaplan. In addition, the final version of this text was reviewed by trainer, Sharon Carlstrom, an American Council on Exercise and the Aerobic Fitness Association of America certified personal trainer and group exercise instructor and member of the American College of Sports Medicine and by Lisa Lewis, certified personal trainer, American Council on Exercise. We wish to thank Anthony Better, manager of Gold's Gym for the use of Gold's Gym at the Power Plant in Baltimore, Maryland. Thanks also to our models/trainers: Darrin Carter; Anthony Better, certified personal trainer, ISSA; Lisa Lewis, certified personal trainer, American Council on Exercise; and Laura Liang,

The health, fitness, and nutritional information contained in this book is not intended to be a substitute for medical advice. Consult your physician before starting this or any other fitness program.

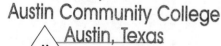
Library Services
Austin Community College
Austin, Texas

Contents

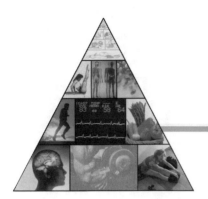

Foreword by
James A. Gondles, Jr., CAE

Physical fitness can save your life. Not only can a regular exercise routine help you stay alive in challenging situations, but it can make you feel more vital. Exercise boosts your spirit so that you can react to stress and tension in your everyday life with greater flexibility.

We all tend to procrastinate—I'll start the program once I have read the book. You can begin exercising before you have completed your reading. This is your book. Use it to make notations on your progress. Write down how you are feeling. List how many repetitions you can do each day. Then, a few months from now, see how much progress you have made.

Those who are knowledgeable about fitness and simply want an exercise program can start reading Chapter 10. Those who need some persuasion should start at the beginning. The chapters on health and nutrition present much information that may become more useful once you begin to exercise.

This program works no matter who you are—no matter what your age. In fact, exercise can help you feel younger. You can exercise without expensive equipment. The author goes through all the excuses and rationalizations and offers some concrete and convincing evidence that you, too, can be fit.

James A. Gondles, Jr., CAE
Executive Director
American Correctional Association

Introduction:
Why Concern Ourselves with Fitness?

The sources of stress in the corrections profession are legion, and it takes its toll, but you can do something about it. One way of combating the effects of stress is through a systematic program of exercise and diet.

After you get off your shift, following either an extremely active shift or a miserably boring one, you often just want to sit down in front of your television, elevate your feet, and . . . "meditate." Perhaps after awhile, you begin to ask yourself some very important personal questions, such as, "Is this what life is all about?" or "Is there life after the walls?" Yes, there *is*! But, YOU have to take the responsibility to find it! The quality of life that you are looking for is obtainable. However, it is up to YOU to grab onto it! And, becoming physically fit is one way you can do it for yourself.

This fitness program was developed for both correctional and law enforcement personnel to follow and use as a self-help remedy for many of our "self-inflicted" problems. It can be used by both men and women of all ages.

There are many benefits of being physically fit. However, just because a person is physically fit, does not necessarily mean that he or she never will be injured. However, research on athletes who are injured indicates that they generally will recover from their injury much faster than an unfit person due to their level of fitness. This should demonstrate that if we get injured, we also should have the same ability to recover more quickly if we are at a higher level of fitness at the time of our injury.

CHAPTER 1:

Physical Fitness in Corrections and Law Enforcement

As anyone in corrections knows and the National Institute of Corrections confirms, the job of a correctional officer involves more than simply following the policies and procedures of your respective facility. Correctional officers have positive as well as negative interactions with inmates daily that are totally unpredictable and sometimes dangerous. As a result, officers constantly feel the effects of their high-stress profession.

Correctional officers have an important role in achieving the goals of corrections, including protecting the public and assisting offenders by helping them to improve their lives. They also need to think about ways of achieving their personal maximum potential in all aspects of their profession and personal life. Such training among other things should include: physical techniques for safely handling inmates, stress awareness, and a systematic physical exercise program for themselves that also includes a well-designed nutritional education program.

Many state departments of correction are concerned about their employees' health and fitness. In their Employee Wellness Program, the Washington State Department of Corrections recommended that their employees moderately exercise for thirty minutes or more on most if not all days. They stated that "moderate exercise" included walking briskly, washing the windows or the car, mowing the lawn or raking the leaves, or playing ball with the kids. Their employees have discovered that regular exercise makes them stronger and more energetic and that it reduces the effects of stress.

A study conducted by the International Association of Chiefs of Police (IACP) (1997) regarding physical fitness concerns in law enforcement, which also applies to corrections, determined that agency fitness programs should cover four major areas: (1) aerobic power, (2) strength, (3) flexibility, and (4) body composition. Correctional and law enforcement wellness programs also should include motor ability and skill activities, too.

The IACP study found that these abilities and skills included:
- Speed (speed in muscular movement)

- Coordination (the ability to walk, talk, and chew gum at the same time)
- Balance (the ability to maintain your equilibrium in movement)
- Agility (the ability to put one foot in front of the other without tripping yourself)
- Performance of specific motor acts, such as, using a baton and restraints

Fitness and health-related problems associated with corrections and law enforcement are a "double-edged sword" and the corrections and law enforcement community, as a whole, have significant health and disability risk problems that are job-specific to the profession. In fact, the rate of workers' compensation claims in corrections and law enforcement was six times that of the national average for workers' compensation type injuries.

The IACP study found the following examples of physical risk problems of those in corrections and law enforcement included a high coronary risk profile with a high rate of premature deaths due to chronic heart disease and a high rate of diseases stemming from a lack of exercise, such as back pain. There was a very high rate of early retirement and disability due to these same issues: 22 percent of the early retirements or disabilities were due to back problems while 26 percent were due to cardiovascular problems. Almost a fifth had psychological problems.

On-duty deaths that were health related accounted for 60 percent of the total of all on-duty deaths. Off-duty deaths that were health related were 21 percent of the total. There also were high rates of stress disorders, such as alcoholism and divorce. Among this group, there was a low fitness level compared to the general population and compared with the inmate population.

Those in corrections and law enforcement exhibited a poor lifestyle—only 14 percent were active. More than 60 percent smoked. And 60 percent were overweight. Table 1.1 shows the injuries that led to disability.

Table 1.1: Significant Injuries Leading to Disability

Back—	17.2 percent	Neck—	8.1 percent
Ankles—	13.2 percent	Legs—	6.5 percent
Knees—	13.0 percent	Shoulders—	5.7 percent
Wrists—	11.8 percent		

Source: IACP (1997)

There is some good news. There is a national trend supporting a massive movement towards employee health promotion. In this regard, the correctional and law enforcement community gradually is catching-up with the rest of the nation. From 1980 to 1990, the number of joggers increased in America from approximately 100,000 to about 3,000,000. During approximately the same time period, American corporations spent an estimated seven billion dollars annually on employee fitness problems. Becoming healthier and more physically fit are important goals for individuals in corrections and law enforcement.

Fitness of employees has an economic payoff for the agency or corporation.

- Reduced health and life insurance premiums if employees maintain a certain level of fitness
- Reduced absenteeism
- Reduced health care claims
- Greater productivity

Increasingly, there is a no-smoking policy for hiring, which means a healthier workforce. Based on these factors, good fitness becomes an economic issue. Physical fitness is also a readiness issue. Good fitness minimizes known risks.

Fitness readiness involves increasing an individual's specific and general readiness. *Specific readiness* includes an individual's stamina, power to implement the use of force, the ability to stretch and use a full range of motion, and a generalized category of general movement. *General readiness* includes an individual's physiological mobilization efficiency, which translates to an individual's functional work capacity and recovery. General readiness means an increased tolerance of fatigue, and an increased alertness. It also includes increased safety and physical performance. This results in the lowering of the risk of injury and an increase in the ability to perform, increased survivability, and a lower safety risk to others.

Without fitness, individuals have an increased risk of not being physiologically ready. This can result in harm to themselves, to others, to their community, to their mission, and can result in charges of negligence against an individual and coworkers.

Additionally, there is a personal cost to poor fitness—an increased risk to one's health. This may result in a disability, a coronary risk, greater stress, less movement efficiency, and consequently, greater injury and less physical and emotional well-being. This means that the individual's heart and blood vessels are not working as well as they should and the individual has a greater overall disease risk, a tendency to obesity, and a lowered positive psychological status.

By contrast, people who are physically fit present less of a problem in risk management. They are absent less, spend less on health care costs, and have greater productivity.

The IACP study (1997) also determined the value of physical training and its effects on the members of the corrections and law enforcement community. The study found the following:

- Physical training had an impact on an individual's health. This included improvement in an individual's heart and the vascular system, blood pressure, blood lipids (cholesterol), the lungs and respiration, body composition and weight, the muscle system, the bones, and the endocrine system.
- There also were improvements in emotional factors. This involved a lessening of anxiety and depression, improved self-esteem, a feeling of general well-being, greater emotional stability, and less impact of stress.

- There were positive effects on job-related factors. This included improvement in the amount of absenteeism, lower health care costs, less turnover, greater ease in training, increased productivity, and increased job performance ratings.

After studying 1,389 law enforcement employees in the United States who had participated in a progressive physical fitness program, the IACP study (1997) discovered the following interesting results:

- There was a 22 percent increase in participants' fitness.
- Participants' disability days decreased by 20.1 percent.
- Participants' direct disability dollar costs decreased by 31.7 percent.
- Participants had 42.6 fewer disability days than nonparticipants.
- Participants' major medical costs were lowered by 45.7 percent.
- The annual cost per participant was $120.
- The annual savings per participant was $353.
- The annual savings difference was $232.78, which is 66 percent less than nonparticipants.

Stress

Few professions in the world place a person in life-threatening situations as often as corrections. Every day, we experience situations and do things that the ordinary citizen would never imagine. For example, how many ordinary citizens are thrown into potentially violent situations or are forced to defend themselves against a combatant in an assaultive altercation?

The Washington State Department of Corrections defines "stress" as a natural reaction of the body to any demand (pleasant or unpleasant) placed upon it. Although physical demands, such as removing ourselves from dangerous encounters with inmates, are definite "stressors," psychological demands, such as worry, deadlines, promotions, and so forth, are also major stressors in today's competitive society.

In addition, if there is one universal complaint among correctional staff, it is the issue of job-related stress. All people experience a certain amount of personal stress in their daily living. In fact, some degree of stress actually may be beneficial, since a totally stress-free life would become a boring routine. We all have a different internal ability to cope with our stress. However, when stressful conditions on the job exceed one's ability to cope, then debilitating effects emerge. These include poor health, increased safety problems, and a drop in job performance. After a while, we are torn—both physically and emotionally. We soon learn that we must discover our personal outlets and our "places" for escape.

Research has revealed that it is often not inmates but other members of staff who are more chronically stress inducing. Thus, on-sight operational coworkers, first-line supervisors, managers, and administrators are the people who may raise your stress level. One study revealed that correctional officers actually outranked inmates in terms of creating continual pressures and problems. Furthermore, in terms of how they are treated by supervisors, many indicate that they either are not recognized or are given attention only when something goes wrong.

Additional research confirms that the difficulty of working in correctional facilities is related more to the problems involving staff relationships than to problems in dealing with inmates. Interactions with other officers heighten stress. Even when officer-inmate interactions have been identified as a major source of stress inducement, the underlying cause for the stress has been attributed to administrative problems such as unclear guidelines, inadequate communication, conflicting orders, and the lack of opportunity to participate in the decision-making process. In fact, according to one study, the lack of administrative support ranked among the highest sources of stress in corrections.

Recent data, also, suggests that correctional personnel have indicated that the physical cost of working in the field of corrections is extremely high. Correctional officers are more likely to suffer from an increased likelihood of heart attacks, ulcers, and hypertension than any other professional in similar fields. It is also interesting to note that the life span for correctional personnel is greatly reduced. Studies have indicated that the average life span for a correctional officer is fifty-nine years of age as opposed to the national average life span of seventy-five years of age. The same studies have shown that high rates of alcoholism, suicide, and marital/family difficulties are prevalent among correctional personnel. These studies have indicated that the divorce rate for correctional officers is about twice the divorce rate for the nation, according to data from the National Institute of Corrections.

The question then may be asked—why is a career in corrections so stressful that officers die at an earlier age and have twice the divorce rate than in most other professions? There are many reasons for this occurrence that will be covered later in this book. However, needless to say, correctional officers must endure a more negative environment daily than many others. What other career places its employees with convicted felons on an everyday basis? What other careers lock their employees up behind the same steel doors and bars as dangerous felons? What other careers place their employees in the presence of criminals where violence is the normal way of life?

Those in corrections know it is a very stressful occupation. Some officers may experience in their first year of service what most citizens could experience in a lifetime. Stress is a part of all jobs, and the corrections professional must learn how to accept it or leave the profession. This learning curve about stress includes bursting several myths. These myths include the following:

Myth: Each of us knows when we are under stress.
Fact: Rarely do we know. We simply get used to the feeling.

Myth: Stress affects only those involved with high-pressure jobs.
Fact: Everyone, young and old, is affected by stress.

Myth: The events that happen to us cause stress.
Fact: No. Our interpretation of an event is what causes stress.

Myth: Emotions cannot be controlled.

Fact: Not true. You can control unhappiness and anger just as you create enthusiasm and happiness.

Scientists indicate that stress is the general, nonspecific response of the body to physical changes produced by any stimulus. The stimulus may be pleasant or it may be unpleasant. In either event, with stress the following bodily changes may occur:

- The hormone adrenaline is secreted from the adrenal gland.
- The heart rate increases.
- The pupils of the eyes enlarge.
- The body temperature rises.
- Blood pressure rises.
- The liver releases stored sugar into the blood.
- The breathing rate increases.
- Muscular strength increases.

Together, these changes are known as *the stress response*. A stimulus that results from these changes is referred to as a *stressor*. The stressor may be anything that causes the body to respond. The stress response is also called the *fight or flight* response. Imagine receiving a call from your supervisor to come into the facility immediately because there is a violent situation occurring. Immediately, the stress response occurs. Physical changes begin to take place, such as the release of adrenaline and an increase in your heart and breathing rates. You are ready to either fight or take flight. Either way, you attempt to protect yourself.

Correctional officers could face stress from many origins. Some stress origins include the following things:

- A change in assignment
- Pressure to achieve goals
- Feelings of inadequacy
- Someone always wanting some of your time
- Being blamed for your failures
- Being in a hostile environment

Go ahead, name some other sources of stress in your life:

_____

_____

_____

_____

_____

_____

_____

_____

Some of the worst sources of stress are those over which we feel powerless. Correctional officers experience the fight/flight response and the bodily changes that occur as a result of the response on a constant basis. Some very specific correctional stressors that cause this response to occur are the following:

- Role conflict
- Inconsistent organizational procedures
- Fear for personal safety
- Lack of career development
- Excessive paperwork
- Encouragement for poor job performance
- Isolation
- Daily uncertainty
- Social pressures
- Staff conflicts
- Press and court attitudes and pressures
- Poor organizational communications

Unless we find constructive ways to adapt to the changes we experience, our body will suffer. In fact, any part of our body can be damaged by excessive, unrelieved stress. High blood pressure, kidney disease, peptic ulcers, asthma, headaches, endocrine gland disorders, heart conditions, destructive off-work habits, sour attitude, excessive sick time, more than usual impatience, feelings of being alone, headaches, and stomach aches are all believed to have their beginnings in excessive stress. And once such a condition is established, it becomes a stressor itself. This adds to the problem, making it even more difficult to treat.

Obesity, alcoholism, drug abuse, excessive smoking, and even common colds sometimes can be traced back to excessive stress. Some medical experts believe that as many as 70 percent of today's health problems are the result of excessive stress. In the past few years, noninfectious diseases such as heart disease, cancer, and respiratory disease have taken more lives than infectious diseases. Stress is believed to be a strong factor in causing these noninfectious diseases.

Your body will inform you that you are experiencing a problem that you must deal with or suffer the consequences later. Some of the early stress signals that you might experience could include the following:

- Tension/nervousness
- "Edgy" feelings
- Worrying about trivial matters
- Sleeplessness
- Minor physical ailments
- Interpersonal difficulties with relationships
- Hypersensitivity
- Overly emotional behavior
- Frequent mood changes
- Accident proneness
- Frequent loss of temper

After a period of time, you may experience more serious signals that your stress has become all consuming. That is, if you fail to deal with the stress signals that you have early, you will experience more severe stress signals later. The following are some of the stress signals that you could experience:

- Growing anxiety
- Reckless behavior
- Difficulty with simple tasks
- Exaggerated fear of death

- Feelings of fear and guilt
- Overly suspicious behavior
- Impaired judgment
- Extreme loss of temper
- Violence toward all

Healthy people can cope with stress more easily and effectively than those who are not healthy. Every action you take to promote good health for yourself also promotes your ability to cope with stress. Here are some things that promote good health practices:

- Adequate diet—it takes good nutrition to be able to stand up to the demands of daily stressors.
- Exercise—not only is exercise essential to good physical health, it is also beneficial to social and mental health.
- Sleep—the changes that occur in the body during sleep are almost opposite those of stress. In other words, the heart rate decreases, blood pressure lowers, your temperature decreases, and the body renews itself to cope with the stressors of the next day.
- Relaxation—relaxing completely once a day is good for both physical and mental health.
- Physical checkups—it is difficult to deal with stress when you are ill. Regular physical checkups can identify symptoms of illness before they become serious.

There are other general ways of coping with stress. We all must find what works best for us. Some additional ideas include the following suggestions:

- Work off stress.
- Talk out your worries.
- Learn to accept what you cannot change.
- Balance work and recreation.
- Do something for others.
- Take one thing at a time.
- Give in once in a while.
- Make yourself available to others.

Do all of these lists regarding stress and its effects sound familiar to you? Probably, you have heard all this before, but did it penetrate enough to get you to do something differently? If you conscientiously will try, exercise, fitness, and good nutrition can help you, too.

When it comes right down to it, doing something about your stress depends on you. What do you like to do? What are you going to do about your stress? Will you use positive or negative ways to cope with it?

Here is one more list for you to think about. It is entitled "Positive personal management ideas for stress reduction." The following list is a positive approach:

- Be yourself.
- Know your own capabilities and tolerances of stress.
- Know your own limitations.
- Learn to say "no."
- Be active every day.
- Plan some idleness every day.
- Maintain your "ideal" weight.
- Avoid between-meal snacks.
- Read books requiring concentration.

- Stay in touch with yourself.
- Communicate your feelings with others.
- Be honest with yourself and others.
- Be in control of yourself.
- Get help if or when you need it.
- Always think positively.
- Avoid irritating, overly competitive people.
- Plan leisurely, less-structured vacations.
- Live by the calendar, not by the stopwatch.

There are several negative coping techniques that you need to avoid. Although it is easy to fall into the "trap," consider dealing with your stress using positive coping methods. Negative coping methods include the following:

- Smoking
- Overeating
- Abusing alcohol
- Abusing chemicals
- Taking your emotions out on your family
- Biting your fingernails
- Getting sick all of the time

Physical Condition

As a result of stress and lack of physical conditioning, a large number of correctional officers are in terrible physical condition, and the stress of the job is literally killing them! The longer they have been away from an academy, the worse the physical condition they are likely to have. In most correctional agencies, physical training is strictly voluntary and little is ever said regarding an officer's poor physical condition. Officers may tell themselves that they are fit enough, but many, when faced with a physical altercation with an inmate (who is, by the way, generally in much better physical condition than the average officer), would fall flat on their faces before they are able to successfully make it out of the altercation.

Fitness establishes presence. Inmates may not want to bother a fit officer. According to Dennis Hutchinson (2000), an out-of-shape officer who is seriously hypertensive or has other significant health problems may be at substantial risk of a heart attack, stroke, or other serious medical problems if he [or she] is forced to suddenly engage in intensive aggressive, physical exertions such as:

- Subduing a combative prisoner
- Defending him or herself or a fellow officer
- Carrying an unconscious person in an evacuation from a cell fire
- Other arduous physical activity

Mr. Hutchinson continues, in Utah, some agencies are doing fitness testing on a regular basis using a skills-based fitness test, such as obstacle course, fence jump, sprint, and other activities to replicate essential job functions. He asks the question—what happens to those officers who do not pass the test? How much time should be allotted to officers to come into compliance? He notes that the Utah Department of Corrections is considering an option in which officers voluntarily would take a fitness test during annual inservice training. Those who pass the test would receive a nominal incentive award and an achievement ribbon for their uniform (Hutchinson, 2000).

Obesity

Obesity is another important consideration. According to the U.S. Department of Agriculture, people are considered obese when they are approximately 20 percent above their highest body-weight range on a reputable height/weight chart, such as shown in Tables 1.2. and 1.3

According to the U.S. Department of Agriculture, obesity is considered one of the most serious problems in America today. An estimated 15,000,000 Americans are obese to the extent that their health is in jeopardy. Obesity is associated with the onset and progression of hypertension, diabetes, heart disease, and gallbladder disease. Our sedentary lifestyle is considered a contributing factor in the incidence of obesity in this country.

Physical exercise is important for maintaining an ideal body weight and good muscle tone. As we grow older, we require fewer calories to maintain an ideal body weight (*see* Chapter 2). Identifying and changing eating behavior is often the key to permanent weight control. Many people overeat by eating too fast. Skipping meals during the day often results in evening eating binges. Many people overeat by using food to deal with anxieties, frustrations, and boredom. Regular exercise not only burns up excess calories, but also can help relieve tensions, which often lead to overeating.

An officer's sedentary lifestyle may lead to additional stress and unneeded weight. It is easy to leave your shift and vegetate when you get home. After all, you may have had a horrible shift and you need to relax. However, instead of going straight home, have you ever thought about going straight to the gym? A good workout will take away much of the stress that you felt when you left your shift. It will cause you to refocus your attention on something other than the encounters you experienced earlier at work. If not a formal workout, an officer might choose to play a game of basketball with others. That is a great start! The officer is choosing something other than nothing, but it also can be devastating to his or her body, including the muscles, joints, connective tissues, and the heart. The once-in-a-while athlete is okay, but the body ends up suffering. Over time, an officer may experience pain, injury, and, maybe even a fatal heart attack.

In the last few years, we have learned much about exercise and its effects on the body. We now know that good, systematic exercise is important in combating some of the most serious, common physical problems and complaints that plague the corrections profession. In other words, fitness should be "proactive" not "fitness by crisis." You should not wait to have a problem before you decide to deal with it. In the corrections and law enforcement professions, we are faced with physical situations that can cause pain, injury, and physical ailments. We must exercise those parts of the body that can cause us the most problems. Some of these physical ailments include the following:

- Lower back pain. There are a number of possible causes of back problems ranging from evolutionary issues to simply the lack of tone in back muscles. When the muscles in this area of the body are strong, conditioned, and flexible, they do a much better job of supporting the vertebrae and keeping them in proper alignment and, thus, eliminating a number of low back complications. They also improve our ability to move.

Table 1.2: Height and Weight Table for Men

Height Feet Inches	Small Frame	Medium Frame	Large Frame
5′2″	128–134	131–141	138–150
5′3″	130–136	133–143	140–153
5′4″	132–138	135–145	142–156
5′5″	134–140	137–148	144–160
5′6″	136–142	139–151	146–164
5′7″	138–145	142–154	149–168
5′8″	140–148	145–157	152–172
5′9″	142–151	148–160	155–176
5′10″	144–154	151–163	158–180
5′11″	146–157	154–166	161–184
6′0″	149–160	157–170	164–188
6′1″	152–164	160–174	168–192
6′2″	155–168	164–178	172–197
6′3″	158–172	167–182	176–202
6′4″	162–176	171–187	181–207

Weights at ages 25–59 based on lowest mortality. Weight in pounds according to frame (in indoor clothing weighing 5 lbs.; shoes with 1" heels). Copyright 1996, 1999. Used by permission of Metropolitan Life Insurance Company, New York.

- Headaches. As we already have discussed, some headaches are due to stress. Tension accumulates in the neck and shoulders and blood vessels are constricted. Eventually, pain occurs. In most cases, the physical release of exercise can help to alleviate this buildup of stress.

- Heart disease. There are a number of forms of heart disease. Many seem to be genetically induced or related to other variables that are difficult to control. However, substantial evidence shows that exercise, with its effects on the heart and circulatory system, can lower the risk of cardiac problems.

- Pulled muscles. There is nothing more disturbing than wrestling on the ground with a combative inmate and suddenly finding yourself suffering from the pain of a strain, sprain, or muscle pull. Many of these injuries, even the minor ones, come about simply because the body has been allowed to degenerate due to lack of use. When you are in better condition, when the muscles are firm and strong, the joints, ligaments, and tendons are flexible, and there is much less chance that you will incur this type of injury.

- Insomnia. Of the many possible causes of insomnia, one is living the kind of life where you build up tension through mental effort, but get no physical release through a comparable effort of the body. People were not meant to just

Table 1.3: Height and Weight Table for Women

Height Feet Inches	Small Frame	Medium Frame	Large Frame
4'10"	102–111	109–121	118–131
4'11"	103–113	111–123	120–134
5'0"	104–115	113–126	122–137
5'1"	106–118	115–129	125–140
5'2"	108–121	118–132	128–143
5'3"	111–124	121–135	131–147
5'4"	114–127	124–138	134–151
5'5"	117–130	127–141	137–155
5'6"	120–133	130–144	140–159
5'7"	123–136	133–147	143–163
5'8"	126–139	136–150	146–167
5'9"	129–142	139–153	149–170
5'10"	132–145	142–156	152–173
5'11"	135–148	145–159	155–176
6'0"	138–151	148–162	158–179

Weights at ages 25–59 based on lowest mortality. Weight in pounds according to frame (in indoor clothing weighing 3 lbs.; shoes with 1" heels). Copyright 1996, 1999. Used by permission of Metropolitan Life Insurance Company, New York.

sit around thinking and worrying. Exercise has a definite effect on the human psychology and often can help to solve or reduce a number of mind-related problems.

- Obesity. Generally, overweight people exercise less than thin ones. Exercise not only burns up more calories in the body, but it also has some kind of an effect on the appetite regulation mechanism in the body. This is another reason that exercise is very helpful in controlling your weight.

Physical fitness is relevant to staying alive in corrections. Effective defensive techniques require dexterity, strength, agility, and suppleness. To cope with the physical exertion under stress that is common with physical encounters, one needs a well-tuned cardiovascular system, quick reflexes, and coordination. All this is possible through exercise.

Cardiovascular Problems

Recent research has shown several factors contribute to the high rate of cardiovascular disease among correctional personnel. They include the following:

- Smoking
- High blood pressure
- Obesity
- A sedentary lifestyle
- Job-related stress

We already have discussed high blood pressure, job-related stress, and a sedentary lifestyle. We now turn to smoking. Obesity is considered in more detail in Chapter 2. Some of the research presented here may surprise you and help you to begin your own fitness campaign.

Smoking

You probably do not want to hear about your smoking—again. However, giving up smoking is extremely important for your health and general well-being. The power that smoking has over a person who smokes long has been recognized. Only recently, investigative research has revealed that nicotine is the material in tobacco that the user craves. Cigarette smoke also contains nicotine, which is the material that causes an intense desire to smoke. Nicotine is a stimulant. It causes your blood pressure and your heart rate greatly to increase. Taken in large doses, nicotine can be poisonous.

Smoke formed by a burning cigarette contains more than 500 different gases. Many of these are known as *carcinogens*—that is, they are cancer producing. Others are called *cocarcinogens*. This means that they are harmless in themselves, but they help to increase the harmful effects of the carcinogens.

More than 90 percent of cigarette smoke is made up of twelve gases that are health hazards. The most dangerous gas in cigarette smoke is carbon monoxide. In the body, carbon monoxide takes the place of some of the oxygen in the blood. Due to carbon monoxide, the heart must work harder to circulate blood so that all body tissues get the necessary amounts of oxygen.

When the particles in cigarette smoke cool, they form a brown, sticky material known as *tar*. The majority of known carcinogens in cigarette smoke are found in tar. Tar builds up in the body, along the air passages leading to the lungs and in the lungs themselves.

Cardiovascular diseases are the most frequent cause of death among smokers. The most important of these diseases include heart attack, atherosclerosis, and stroke. A heart attack is the most prevalent cause of death among cigarette smokers. Smokers have twice the risk of heart attack as nonsmokers.

People who suffer a heart attack also may suffer from atherosclerosis. In atherosclerosis, deposits gradually build up on the inner walls of the arteries. The deposits are made of fatty substances, including cholesterol. If deposits clog the arteries that nourish the heart, the heart does not receive enough oxygen and nutrients. As a result, cells of the heart die and a heart attack occurs. The arteries of smokers contain more cholesterol than those of nonsmokers. In addition, a smoker's heart needs to work harder because nicotine causes the arteries to constrict. The heart is overworked trying to pump blood through restricted arteries. Blood flow to vital organs may be cut off and death may occur.

Smoking also causes the formation of blood clots. As a result of these blood clots, the flow of blood through the arteries may become blocked. If a blood clot forms in an artery that nourishes the heart, death may result. Blood clots occur more frequently in the arteries of smokers than in nonsmokers. Due to the already stressful nature of corrections and law enforcement, people in these professions should cut down their smoking and eventually, eliminate it all together.

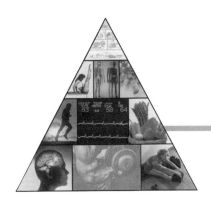

CHAPTER 2:
Nutrition and Diet Programs

All foods are made up of nutrients. Nutrients are substances the body needs to carry on life processes. Hundreds of different nutrients have been identified. However, because many are similar in content and function, they can be grouped together. There are six main kinds of nutrients:

- Carbohydrates
- Proteins
- Minerals
- Fats
- Vitamins
- Water

Foods contain nutrients in different amounts. To nourish your body, a food must supply nutrients that do at least one of the following: provide fuel for energy, provide materials for building or maintaining body tissue, or provide substances that act to regulate body processes.

Some foods provide all six kinds of nutrients, while others provide only one or two. Most foods have at least tiny amounts of all the nutrients, though some may be unusually rich in one but poor in another. You need nutrients of each kind every day. However, your needs are greatest for proteins, carbohydrates, fats, and water. You need only tiny amounts of vitamins and minerals, but these nutrients are still crucial to life and health.

Taken as a whole, the foods you eat every day must supply nutrients to nourish your body. Eating nutritious foods will help you look good, feel good, resist stress and disease, and have vitality and joy in living.

Foods filled with nutrients used to supply energy are carbohydrates and fats. Such foods should supply a little more than half of your daily diet. The main carbohydrates in foods are sugars and starches. Milk, dried fruit, fruit juices, honey, and syrup all have a high sugar content. Sugar is also found in such vegetables as carrots, beets, winter squash, and turnips. Good sources of starch are grains and all products made from grains, as well as beans, peas, and potatoes.

Many foods that contain carbohydrates also provide cellulose. Cellulose makes up the fibrous parts of plants such as leaves, stems, roots, seeds, and fruit skins. This material is not digested and, therefore, is not a source of energy. However, it does provide roughage or bulk. Roughage helps food and wastes move through your system. This is important for regular elimination.

For most people, a diet totally without fats would be dry and unappetizing. The flavor of vegetables and meats, for example, often is enhanced by fats such as oils, margarine, butter, and salad dressings. Olives, avocados, nuts, milk, and cheese are other sources of fats. In the body, fats provide a concentrated source of energy.

Fats that are eaten and are not used immediately by the body are stored as body fat. Much of it is stored directly under the skin, giving shape to your body. Other stored body fat forms a protective cushion around your vital body organs. Fats also help keep the skin from becoming dry and flaky.

Next to water, the most abundant substance in the human body is protein. The largest portion is found in muscle tissue. Protein is also part of other soft tissues and of blood, bones, and teeth. In fact, protein is an essential part of every cell.

You supply protein to body cells by eating foods that contain protein. Protein is then used to build new cells in muscles, blood, bones, teeth, hair, and glands. Protein also is used to maintain and repair existing cells. Protein is needed to produce enzymes and hormones, substances which regulate many chemical changes in the body. If the diet lacks enough carbohydrates or fats, protein may be used to provide energy.

Body protein and protein in foods you eat are complex combinations of amino acids. The body breaks down protein you eat into amino acids. These amino acids then are used to build new cells and maintain cells that already are formed. Many different amino acids are needed to form protein. Some can be made in the body. Others, considered essential, must be provided in the foods that you eat. Adults need less protein than growing children. In adults, protein primarily is used for maintenance and repair. A lack of protein affects the entire body and may cause diseases.

A diet high in animal protein is often high in extra saturated fat, cholesterol, and calories. The average American tends to eat approximately twice the amount of protein generally recommended. Excessive consumption of protein many tax your kidneys, which rid the body of the extra protein and nitrogen it does not need. Protein requirements are high during growth, pregnancy, lactation, and stress (including surgery, fever, infection, and injury).

Vitamins are substances in foods that are essential for body processes. Vitamins do not provide energy or body building materials. However, they work with each other, with other nutrients, and with other substances to regulate body functions. Vitamins promote normal digestion and help the body use proteins, fats, and carbohydrates. They promote normal growth and help the body resist infections. Everyone needs to eat foods that contain vitamins and minerals. If you do not eat enough of any one vitamin, disease may result. Several diseases are caused by a lack of one or more vitamins. Eating a balanced diet will take care of this problem.

Some people believe everyone needs to take vitamin supplements each day. For most people, food is the best source of vitamins and minerals. Supplements should be taken only on the advice of your physician. Remember, it is not possible to store all the needed vitamins in your body. For example, your body only will use the amount of vitamin C it needs in a single day. What is not needed is passed out of the body.

And, taking extra large amounts of certain vitamins can be toxic to your body. For example, too much vitamin A may cause a variety of reactions, including liver damage. Too much vitamin D can cause pain, stiffness, and damage to the soft tissues.

Chart 2.1 represents the types of vitamins and functions they have on the human body, and some food sources that are considered good for them:

Chart 2.1 Vitamins

Vitamin	Function in the body	Food Sources
A	Helps develop and maintain healthy skin, hair, and mucous membranes Helps prevent eye disorders Aids in resisting infections	Whole milk, liver, green and yellow vegetables, egg yolks, butter, and margarine
B Group B1 Thiamin	Helps release energy from foods Promotes appetite Helps the nerves function Keeps digestive tract healthy	Meats (especially pork), liver, enriched whole grain breads, cereals, legumes, nuts, vegetables, and milk
B2 Riboflavin	Helps maintain skin, eyes, and nerves Helps the body use carbohydrates, fats, and proteins to release energy Essential for healthy offspring	Liver, milk, green leafy vegetables, enriched whole grain breads, cereals, cheese, meats, eggs, and legumes
B6 Pyridoxine	Used in protein metabolism Aids in making red blood cells Helps the nerves function	Meats, poultry, fish, whole grain breads cereals, and potatoes
B12	Needed to produce red blood cells Needed for normal growth of all cells Helps the nervous system function	Meat, fish, eggs, and milk/milk products
Folic acid	Needed to produce RNA, DNA, and normal red blood cells Helps maintain the digestive tract	Liver, green leafy vegetables, legumes, enriched whole grain breads cereals, and nuts
Pantothenic Acid	Aids in metabolism of carbohydrates, fats, proteins	Milk, eggs, enriched whole grain breads, cereals, liver, vegetables, and fruits
Niacin	Aids in producing energy from carbohydrates Helps maintain all body tissues	Enriched whole grain breads and cereals, fish, liver, meat, poultry, and legumes
Biotin	Aids in metabolism of carbohydrates, fats, and proteins	Liver, kidneys, egg yolks, legumes, and nuts

(continued on next page)

Chart 2.1 Vitamins (continued)

C	Aids in healing wounds Helps form and maintain the "cementing" material between cells Essential for healthy teeth and gums Aids in resisting infections Necessary for strong blood vessels	Citrus fruits, berries, melons, tomatoes, potatoes, green peppers, and green leafy vegetables
D	Helps build strong bones and teeth	Milk, fish liver oil, and liver
E	Prevents damage to cell membranes Protects vitamin A	Vegetable oils, margarine, liver, vegetables, and enriched whole grain breads and cereals
K	Promotes normal blood clotting	Green leafy vegetables, peas, and grains

Source: The U.S. Department of Agriculture.

Minerals and vitamins are important to your body because they help regulate and coordinate bodily functions. Minerals occur naturally on the earth, in soil, and in water. Many minerals have been identified in foods and are considered necessary in your diet. Minerals provide important body building materials. They regulate many body processes.

The U.S. Department of Agriculture developed Chart 2.2 to explain the minerals people need, their function in the body and food sources where they are found.

Chart 2.2: Minerals

Mineral	Function in the Body	Food Sources
Calcium	Builds and maintains teeth and bones Helps blood to clot Helps nerves and muscles to function	Milk, cheese, and green leafy vegetables
Phosphorus	Combines with calcium to build and maintain teeth and bones Helps nerves and muscles to function	Milk, cheese, whole grains, nuts, liver, fish, eggs, and poultry
Magnesium	Activates many enzyme reactions Helps make proteins Helps body to use calcium and phosphorus	Red meat, potatoes, nuts, corn, green leafy vegetables, and cereals
Iron	Combines with protein to make hemoglobin Aids in growth of muscles, glands, and nerves	Liver, red meat, egg yolks, dried fruits, enriched cereals, green leafy vegetables, nuts, and legumes
Iodine	Forms part of hormone secretions of the thyroid gland, which regulates the rate at which foods are burned in the body	Seafood, iodized salt
Copper	Aids in several reactions in the body, such as the making of hemoglobin	Nuts, raisins, liver, kidneys, legumes, and shellfish
Zinc	Necessary for normal taste and smell Aids in general growth of all tissues Aids in healing wounds	Meat, liver, eggs, seafood, milk, and whole grains

Water

Water is essential for all life! Every cell in the body requires water to carry on its functions. Oxygen is the only substance that is more important to life than water. And water must be continuously supplied to make up for the water that is used and lost in keeping the body functioning. Water is supplied in milk, soups, juices, and in juicy fruits and vegetables such as tomatoes, melons, and lettuce. We should drink eight to ten glasses of water each day. Drink even more if you exercise hard. Water is lost through sweat. The American Dietetic Association (2000) notes, "increased muscular activity leads to an increase in heat production in the body; this is dissipated, in part through the production of sweat. To prevent dehydration, water must be replaced at a faster rate. Dehydration has an adverse effect on muscle strength, endurance, and coordination and increases the risk of cramps, heat exhaustion, and life-threatening heat stroke."

For most individuals who exercise one hour or less per day, water is the best supplement. Some of the commercial sports beverages may promote gastric distress. Carrying around a water bottle with a tip that allows you to pull up on it to get water makes it easy to drink enough.

Benefits of a Balanced Diet

A balanced diet provides all the nutrients you need in their correct amounts. It is important to remember that although one food may contain many nutrients, there is no perfect food that contains all the necessary nutrients. Eating a variety of foods will help you get the nutrients you need. One way to make sure you are eating a good variety of foods is to choose foods from the five major food groups. From day to day, select as many different kinds of food as you can from each group. Be sure that all five food groups are well represented in your daily diet.

There is no magic pill that will allow you to get extra endurance or stamina when you exercise. The American Dietetic Association (2000) notes: "Compounds such a bee pollen, caffeine, glycine, lecithin, brewer's yeast, and gelatin are claimed through anecdotal evidence to improve strength or endurance. Although popular with some athletes because of this perceived benefit, scientific research has failed to substantiate the claims for these products or inadequate research has been undertaken with these supplements." The Association concluded that even though some of these items may provide a psychological benefit, "when use of these substances replaces a sound nutrition program, health and performance may be compromised, resulting in serious consequences."

During digestion, all carbohydrates are broken down into simple sugars. Glucose is the main form of sugar used by your cells. It enters your blood and supplies the cells with energy. The amount of glucose in blood is called the blood sugar level. Muscles need glucose to work properly. When your muscles are not supplied with the necessary amount of glucose, you fatigue.

Eating a high-carbohydrate breakfast—for example, orange juice and toast—will quickly raise your energy level. This is because carbohydrates are digested rapidly. There is a rapid increase in your blood sugar level. When the energy is used up, your blood sugar level falls, and you begin to feel hungry and tired.

Some of the protein you eat is also changed to glucose. However, protein is digested more slowly than carbohydrates, and the glucose is released into the blood at a slower rate. A breakfast that provides protein, such as eggs and milk, as well as carbohydrates will keep you feeling energetic all morning.

For a well-balanced diet, you should try to eat foods from the five major food groups. Your foods should be low in fat, low in sodium, and low in sugar but high in fiber. Another way to think about your diet is through the following caloric intake guidelines: 50 percent carbohydrates, 30 percent fats, and 20 percent proteins.

According to the U.S. Department of Agriculture, the following chart indicates the servings that are necessary for you to develop and maintain a healthy body:

Chart 2.3: Basic Food Groups

A Guide to Daily Food Choices

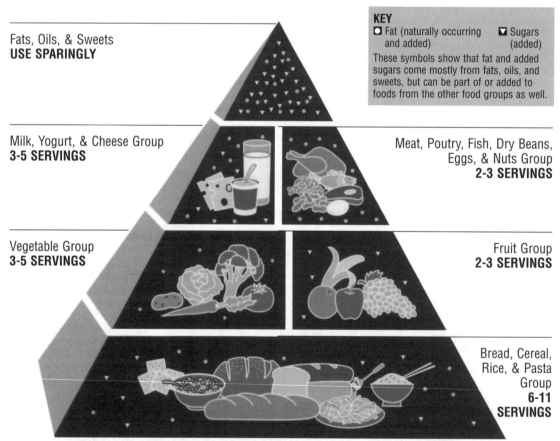

KEY
◻ Fat (naturally occurring and added)   ◪ Sugars (added)

These symbols show that fat and added sugars come mostly from fats, oils, and sweets, but can be part of or added to foods from the other food groups as well.

Fats, Oils, & Sweets
USE SPARINGLY

Milk, Yogurt, & Cheese Group
3-5 SERVINGS

Meat, Poutry, Fish, Dry Beans, Eggs, & Nuts Group
2-3 SERVINGS

Vegetable Group
3-5 SERVINGS

Fruit Group
2-3 SERVINGS

Bread, Cereal, Rice, & Pasta Group
6-11 SERVINGS

Source: U.S. Department of Agriculture/U.S. Department of Health and Human Services

Chart 2.4: What Counts as One Serving?

Breads, Cereals, Rice, and Pasta
1 slice bread
1/2 cupcooked rice or pasta
1/2 cup cooked cereal
1 ounce of ready-to-eat cereal

Vegetable
1/2 cup chopped raw or
   cooked vegetables
1 cup of leafy raw vegetables

Fruit
1 piece of fruit or melon wedge
3/4 cup of juice
1/2 cup of canned fruit
1/4 cup of dried fruit

Milk, Yogurt, and Cheese
1 cup of milk or yogurt
1-1/2 to 2 ounces of cheese

Meat, Poultry, Fish, Dry beans, Eggs, and Nuts
2-1/2 to 3 ounces of cooked lean
   meat, poultry, or fish
Count 1/2 cup of cooked beans or
   1 egg, or 2 tablespoons of
   peanut butter as 1 ounce of
   lean meat (about 1/3 serving)

Fats, Oils, and Sweets
LIMIT CALORIES FROM THESE
especially if you need to lose
weight

The amount you eat may be more than one serving. For example, a dinner portion of spaghetti would count as two or three servings of pasta.

Source: U.S. Department of Agriculture

As we indicated earlier, your diet should consist mainly of the following ratio of food types: 50 percent carbohydrates (mainly complex, as opposed to simple); 30 percent fats (primarily polyunsaturated fats as opposed to saturated fats); and 20 percent proteins (complete proteins consisting of essential amino acids). Your diet plan should be low in fats, sugars, and sodium, but high in fiber. The Department of Agriculture's food guide pyramid provides the outline for healthy eating.

Another element in a sensible eating plan is to watch your portion sizes. *Dietary Guidelines for Americans, 2000* recommends "be especially careful to limit portion size of foods high in calories, such as cookies, cakes, other sweets, French fries, and fats, oils, and spreads." Additionally, the packaging label on food can tell you how many servings it contains. Of course, second helpings of high calorie foods should be avoided. In fact, except for vegetables without any butter or sauce on them, second helpings of all things should be avoided. Be aware that low fat foods do not always mean low calorie foods. Some people think if it is low fat than they can have more of it. This ruins a sensible eating plan.

Other considerations in your diet include the following items:
- Eat enough calories to attain and/or maintain your desired body weight.
- Eat a balanced diet and a variety of foods at each meal.
- Consistently eat three meals a day.
- Eat fewer foods high in cholesterol.
- Eat fewer foods high in fat.
- Substitute polyunsaturated fats for saturated fats as much as possible.
- Eat more complex carbohydrates and less refined, simple sugars.
- Increase your dietary fiber.

- Drink at least eight to ten glasses of water each day.
- Avoid excessive sodium.
- Try to meet your daily requirements for all nutrients.

The U.S. Department of Agriculture suggests that energy output equivalents of food calories may be expressed in minutes of activity for how long food "sits" in our system when doing these activities. Chart 2.5 indicates this information. The last column, the reclining column, illustrates how the food we eat sometimes can give us very little nutritional value if we do not use it properly. While everyone has a different metabolic "burn-off" rate, however, you should use this as an approximate amount of time for food to pass through your system.

Try to keep track of the food you eat on a daily basis. The chart on the next page is a way for you to keep track of, and control, the foods you eat.

Chart 2.5: How Long Food Stays in Your Body

FOOD	CALORIES	WALKING	CYCLING	SWIMMING	RUNNING	RECLINING
Apple, large	101	19	12	9	5	78
Bacon, 2 strips	96	18	12	9	5	74
Beans, green 1c	27	5	3	2	1	21
Beer, 1 glass	114	22	14	10	6	88
Bread/butter	78	15	10	7	4	60
Cake, 2-layer	356	68	43	32	18	274
Carbonated Bev.	106	20	13	9	5	82
Carrot, raw	42	8	5	4	2	32
Cereal w/milk	200	38	24	18	10	154
Cheese, cottage	27	5	3	2	1	21
Cheese, cheddar	111	21	14	10	6	85
Chicken, fried	232	45	28	21	12	78
Cookie, plain	15	3	2	1	1	12
Cookie, choc.	51	10	6	5	3	39
Doughnut	151	29	18	13	8	116
Egg, fried	110	21	13	10	6	85
Egg, boiled	77	15	9	7	4	59
French dress.	59	11	7	5	3	45
Halibut	205	39	25	18	11	158
Ham, 2 slices	67	32	20	15	9	128
Ice cream	193	37	24	17	10	148
Ice cream soda	255	49	31	23	13	196
Gelatin/crm	117	23	14	10	6	90
Mayonnaise	92	18	11	8	5	71

Chart 2.5: How Long Food Stays in Your Body (continued)

FOOD	CALORIES	WALKING	CYCLING	SWIMMING	RUNNING	RECLINING
Milk, 1 glass	166	32	20	15	9	128
Milk, 1 glass skim	81	16	10	7	4	62
Milk shake	421	81	51	38	22	324
Orange, med.	68	13	8	6	4	52
Orange juice, 1 glass	120	23	15	11	6	92
Pancake, syrup	124	24	15	11	6	95
Peach, med.	46	9	6	4	2	35
Peas, green	56	11	7	5	3	43
Pie, apple	377	73	46	34	19	290
Pizza, cheese	180	35	22	16	9	138
Porkchop	314	60	38	28	16	242
Potato chips	108	21	13	10	6	83
Club sandwich	590	113	72	53	30	454
Hamburger	350	67	43	31	18	269
Tuna sandwich	278	53	34	25	14	214
Sherbet	177	34	22	16	9	136
Shrimp, frd	180	35	22	16	9	138
Spaghetti	396	76	48	35	20	305
Steak	235	45	29	21	12	131

How to Maintain Your Present Weight or Lose Weight

You need to establish your caloric level by using the following formula. To maintain your present body weight, calculate fifteen calories for each pound that you weigh. This is the average for a *moderately* active person. For example, if you are moderately active and weigh 150 pounds, you would require approximately 2,250 calories each day to maintain this weight (15 calories/pound x 150 = 2,250). If you are *sedentary* or get very little exercise, multiply your weight by 13. In this case, the 150-pound person would require only 1,950 calories (13 calories/pound x 150 = 1,950) for weight maintenance.

To lose weight, a deficit of 3,500 calories each week is required. Subtract 500 calories each day to lose a pound a week or 1,000 calories each day to lose 2 pounds each week.

Calories

What is a calorie? Calories are units of measurement that show how much energy you receive from the foods you eat. Every food you eat provides you with some energy that enables you to do the things you do every day as seen in the previous chart.

Chart 2.6: Caloric Intake Chart (You may reproduce this chart)

Date:_____ Weight: _____

FOOD	PORTION	CALORIES

Breakfast:

_____

Lunch:

_____

Dinner:

_____

Desserts:

_____

Snacks:

_____

Drinks:

_____

Other:

_____

My Desired Intake Total: _____

Total Caloric Intake for the day: _____

Adjusting Your Diet to Your Needs

You need to adjust your diet to meet your needs. If you are trying to lose a little weight, you should not drink whole milk. Instead, use either 1 percent or skim milk (low in calories and fat). Do not eat french-fried potatoes or other fried foods. On the other hand, if you wanted to gain a few pounds, you might want to drink a couple of glasses of whole milk with each meal. Always try to use your common sense as to what you should eat and how much. Remember, eat 50 percent carbohydrates, 30 percent fat, and 20 percent protein. If you do not know what the make up is of the foods you eat, you may wish to get a book that lists the carbohydrates, fats, and proteins in food.

If you have decided to gain weight, understand: there is only one way to gain weight and that is to eat more food. There are several ways to do this that make it quite simple. Secondly, you must stay with your weight training program and you will find it easy to gain weight. You need to stay with your diet for at least three to four months, along with your weight training program, and you can gain ten to fifteen "healthy" pounds. However, everyone gains and loses weight at a different rate. Persistence is the key!

Ways to Gain Weight

Eat six small meals each day instead of the customary three meals every day.

Never allow yourself to feel hungry.

- Eat before you go to bed. This is a great way to gain weight. You may try to eat a sandwich with milk prior to going to bed. You even could eat a snack in the middle of the night, as well.
- Slow down on your other activities during the day. You cannot expect to gain weight if you are jogging three-to-four miles every day. Too many activities during your day can result in you burning off too many calories.

A common myth is that you can lose valuable muscular size if you go on a diet. In fact, the opposite is true. If you depend entirely on a tape measure or a scale to determine strength and size, it might seem that your muscles are getting smaller, but they are not. Your measuring tape will indicate that you are losing size; however, it is not the muscle size that you are losing. Instead, you are simply losing fat. You can lose one inch of fat off your arms while your muscles are actually growing. This means that you may have lost one inch around your arms (all fat) while increasing your arms by one-half inch of solid muscle (caused by your workout program and consuming an adequately balanced diet).

Tips on Losing Weight

Obtaining muscular strength and size and losing excess body fat is more complex than gaining weight. To gain weight you simply eat more food. While you are attempting to lose weight, you must exercise the correct number of times indicated in your training schedule, regardless of the results you want to obtain. Remember, results will come faster if you continue to exercise consistently.

While you are dieting, you should not fear an occasional fattening food, such as spaghetti or pizza. Studies have shown that an occasional unaccustomed meal of this kind helps you to produce a weight loss. If you eat fattening foods, however, it never should be more than once a week.

Bread is full of calories. If you can cut the bread from your diet, you can eliminate many calories. Instead of using bread for your sandwiches, try using lettuce. The lettuce you choose needs to be crisp. Try placing between the lettuce leaves a slice of meat, tuna, and tomatoes. You will have a sandwich that is filling, but very low in calories. If you do use bread with your sandwiches, always try to get whole wheat bread instead of white bread. Almost all white bread has little nutritional value, however, it has plenty of calories.

You may never have to diet if you can stay away from these foods:

- Bread and crackers
- French-fried potatoes and other fried foods
- Rice
- Whole milk products
- Candy
- Cookies
- Sugar-coated cereals
- Gravy
- Jams and jellies
- Sugar
- Macaroni and cheese and other pasta, including noodles
- Pizza
- Pastry
- Potato chips and other snack foods
- Soft drinks
- Alcohol

These are the biggest enemies of people who have a tendency to gain weight.

Eat foods that are high in nutritional value and as close to their natural state as possible. Try to eat plenty of lean meats, poultry, fish, seafood, eggs, milk, cheese, vegetables, fruits, whole grain products, and juices. Do not "fall" for expensive over-the-counter pills and powders that are supposed to make you lose weight.

The majority of people do not want to believe that being overweight comes from eating more food than your body requires in terms of spent energy. As you grow older, you need fewer calories—as much as 21 percent less from age twenty-five to sixty-five years. As you become less active, you need fewer calories.

To lose weight, eat small servings and omit all second servings. No matter how many calories there are in a serving of food, smaller or fewer servings mean fewer calories.

Substitute lower-calorie foods for higher-calorie foods. However, you do not have to completely take away your favorite high-calorie foods. Just eat them less often and have smaller servings. Budget your caloric intake to allow for special occasions. Save on calories at other meals during the day/week so you can afford extra calories for these events.

Never skip meals. Skipping meals often leads to unplanned snacking. This will lead to more calories than you want as well as less of the nutritional ones that you need.

A diet low in calories still can offer a large variety of foods. If properly followed, this kind of diet literally, can force your body to lose weight.

To control your weight, you will need to control the amount of energy (number of calories) you consume from food and understand the amount of energy you use during exercise and normal activity. Whether you gain or lose weight or remain the same weight depends on how well you balance the calories furnished by the foods you eat against the calories your body uses up. For example, if you consume too many calories, your body quickly gains weight. For every 3,500 calories consumed and not used up, you gain approximately one pound of weight. This pound of weight represents stored food energy in the form of fat. To lose excess fat, you have to use up stored energy. There are three methods to lose this excess fat: (1) Eat less food (fewer calories) to force your body to draw energy from its stored fat (2) increase your activity to use up more energy, and (3) try both! Use both diet and exercise. Track your food intake on Chart 2.6 on page 24, which you may reproduce.

Drugs and Weight Training

Many athletes take creatine to boost their energy and performance because they see it as a natural remedy as opposed to steroids, which are illegal and have many harmful side effects. However, creatine is not without its risks. In fact, few studies have been done on its safety and efficacy. In many people it can cause cramping and diarrhea and other problems. Until its safety has been proven, it probably is better to avoid using it.

The American Dietetic Association (2000) notes that "the use of amino acid and protein supplements by athletes is common, despite the lack of well-controlled clinical studies to justify their use. Even the highest protein requirements can be met easily with a balanced diet that includes a variety of foods. Therefore, excessive protein intake, either through consumption of high protein foods or protein/amino acid supplements is unnecessary, does not contribute to athletic performance or increase muscle mass, and actually may be detrimental to health and athletic performance."

Also, realize that as a correctional professional, you are risking your career and your livelihood if you engage in illegal behavior, including taking illegal drugs even for the purposes of weight training.

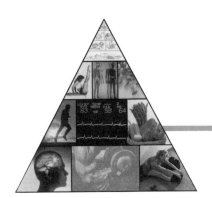

In the last few years, thousands of books have been written about exercise. This is because exercise remains the bargain in the self-help market—especially for those in corrections. The life-enhancing benefits of exercise have been solidly established during the past few years (*see* Chapter 1). Physical exercise is a valuable way for reducing stress and helping officers to become happier, live a healthier lifestyle, and consequently, live a longer and healthier life.

Today, with the surge of interest in physical fitness, certain principles and guidelines do seem to work for everyone in maximizing their efforts. The approach used in this book is simple and it works! In many exercise programs, there is a continuing reluctance to work many muscles, lots of ways at the same time. Therefore, we need to understand that physical fitness is composed of factors that allow us to function effectively physically and mentally while on the job and during our recreation and still have enough energy to handle emergencies. These factors include the following:

- Cardiorespiratory endurance (efficiency with which the body delivers nutrients and oxygen needed for muscular activity and transports waste products from the cells)
- Muscular strength (the greatest amount of force a muscle or a muscle group can exert in one movement). The muscles that support certain joints also will become stronger.
- Muscular endurance (ability of a muscle or muscle group to perform repeated movements with moderate resistance for given period of time).
- Flexibility (ability to move the joints through the entire/normal range of motion). After exercise, your joints may become more stable due to a thickening and strengthening that occurs with strength training.
- Body composition (two major elements—lean body mass, which includes muscle, bone, and essential organ tissue and body fat).

Note: Optimal body composition refers to the proper ratio of body fat to total body weight.

The first four factors have a direct impact on body composition. An important factor in body composition is weight control. Other factors, such as speed, agility, coordination, and balance are properly classified as components of motor fitness.

Principles of Exercise

Correctional exercise consists of certain basic principles that are essential to developing an effective training program. These exercise principles include the following:

- Regularity. Exercise must be performed regularly to provide the training effect. Sporadic exercise may do more harm to the body than good. Regularity is also important in rest, sleep, and in your diet.
- Progression. The intensity of exercise gradually must increase to improve the components of fitness.
- Overload. The workload of each exercise session must exceed normal demands to provide a training effect. However, this does not mean you should overdo the amount you are attempting to lift.
- Balance. Overemphasizing any one of the components of fitness detracts from development of the others. To be effective, an exercise program should include activities that develop all components.
- Variety. Providing a variety of activities reduces boredom and increases motivation.
- Specificity. Training must be geared to the specific improvement desired.
- Recovery. Hard days of training should be followed by easier days to permit recovery. Another way to recover from hard training is to alternate the muscle groups exercised each day.

Your Fitness Goals

Setting Goals. It is important to set goals. They will prevent you from sloughing off on a bad day and skipping exercise. However, set realistic goals so that you do not get discouraged if you do not look like a movie star in a few months and just give up on the whole exercise regime. At the back of the book is a chart that will help you keep track of your exercise. Begin the program as suggested. Then, after you have been doing it for a few weeks, look at your progress and see where you think you will be next month. Set goals that approach becoming fit in a slow and steady measure. Dramatic challenges can harm you and keep you from exercising all together. Write your goals on the chart below. Here are two goals that will help you get started.

Goal #1: Unless you are planning to compete in athletics, your fitness goal should be good health and general well-being.

Goal #2: Always attempt to be as physically fit as the <u>average</u> person you come into contact with on the street or behind the walls.

Your Goals

List your goals and give the date each goal was set. As you make progress in the program, review this list and make changes to it.

_____

_____

_____

_____

_____

_____

_____

_____

_____

_____

_____

_____

_____

_____

_____

Keeping a good diary or log book is important to your success. Record all of your "successes" as well as all of your "failures" in weight training so that you can note what works for you and what does not work for you. While doing this can be a hassle, it is the best and safest way to make your program work. Feel free to use the workout log sheets provided in this book, especially when you decide to move from cycle to cycle in this workout system.

What You Can Expect from the Variable Cyclic Phase System

Most people do not know what to expect from their weight training sessions. For example, it is common to find thin people training in gyms who tell everyone that they only want to become better conditioned, but do not want to become larger. However, realistically speaking, it is very difficult, if not practically impossible, for most people to get "really" big. Normally, it takes many years of intense, determined, goal-oriented, mind-focused work to produce the "perfect" well-conditioned body. Having the right genetic makeup greatly enhances one's potential as well.

Benefits

However, everyone can benefit from weight training. For most people who exercise and lift weights regularly, there is a definite increase in strength and muscular size along with improvement in shape and muscle contour. The body becomes firmer as muscle fibers become more dense and fat is burned off. The body becomes strong, hard, and lean.

Some people may change a lot while others may change somewhat less. Yet, even small changes can make a drastic alteration in your physical conditioning. An inch or two extra around your chest coupled with the loss of a couple of inches around your waist totally can change the way you look and feel.

It is extremely difficult to increase your muscle mass by more than five pounds per year. If you already have had extra muscle mass in the past, it is easier to get it back than to create it in the first place. An extremely well-conditioned athlete may be able to build ten pounds of muscle mass per year, but that is the exception—not the rule.

Aerobic exercises, such as running, swimming, and calisthenics, are referred to as fixed-resistance training. That is, no matter how long you do them, you always are contracting the muscles against the same amount of resistance. You may learn to perform the movements for longer periods of time, which indicates an improvement in your endurance, but you will not become any stronger no matter how many repetitions you perform.

To keep getting stronger, you must increase the resistance so that the muscles continue to adapt. This is referred to as progressive-resistance training, which is the primary principle used in weight training. Each individual can start at his or her own level and make gains on their own schedule. You may be lifting 200 pounds and another person may be lifting 100 pounds, however, so long as you both are lifting to the limit of your strength, both of you essentially are performing an equal amount of work. The objective is to force your muscles to work hard enough to make them adapt.

Muscles

There are three kinds of muscles in our bodies. Each type has its very own characteristics:

- Skeletal Muscles. They are the "system" of long muscles that control the movement of the body. Skeletal muscles make up about 40 percent of most adults' body weight. It is this kind of muscle, under voluntary control, that weight training is designed to strengthen and train.
- Smooth Muscles. They are found in the walls of internal organs, such as the blood vessels, the urinary tract, the gall bladder, the arteries and the veins. These muscles are controlled by the nervous system and hormones. They are not under our conscious control, which is why they are called involuntary muscles.
- Cardiac Muscles. These muscles are located in the tissue that make up the heart. They can be strengthened by cardiovascular, high-repetition exercise.

The function of all muscles is to contract. When we extend or move any muscle in our body in one direction, it takes the contraction of an opposing muscle to bring it back. The more we have trained our muscles, the greater our strength. To increase your strength, you should exercise your major muscles and their opposing muscle. For example, if you exercise your chest, also exercise your upper back. When you exercise your shoulders, exercise your lats. Similarly, when you exercise your biceps, you also should exercise your triceps.

The purpose of our muscles is to overcome the pull of gravity. If we lived on a planet with a stronger gravitational pull, we all would have larger muscles. If, on the other hand, we were living on the moon, which has one-sixth the gravity of Earth, our muscular structure would be correspondingly less. So, the man on the moon would be a dumpy looking guy.

Muscles are highly adaptive. In other words, they change according to the demands placed on them. When we lift a weight or work against some other sort of resistance, in effect, we are creating an artificial gravitational pull. As our muscles are forced to adapt to extra effort, they become stronger and larger. In other words, use a muscle and it gets bigger and stronger—fail to use it and it gets weaker and smaller.

Strength depends on the number of fibers in the muscle and the number of fibers that are involved in any muscular contraction, as well as the strength and thickness of the individual fibers. When contracting a muscle, we use only a percentage of the fibers available to us. If we keep trying to work against heavier amounts of resistance, our body will adapt by causing more of the muscle fibers to contract. This takes time, and there is a physiological limit to this process. However, we get stronger through resistance training that forces our muscles to call on an increased number of muscle fibers to perform the required work. In addition, during exercise, several other beneficial things happen; the muscle fibers become enlarged, the sheath covering the muscles becomes tougher, and the body creates more capillaries to carry blood to the body.

CHAPTER 4.
Weight Training for Women and the Older Worker

The increasing number of women in corrections and law enforcement make these fields more well rounded and professional. Women in corrections and law enforcement must be as physically fit as their male counterparts. However, for many years, weight training had been considered a male activity. For example, men entered body building competitions and strength contests while women only competed in beauty contests where there was little, if any, regard for muscular development. Like much else concerning women, there were a lot of misconceptions.

Here is the truth. Heavy lifting does not result in enlarged muscles that make women "less feminine." In fact, weight training is both the fastest and best way to improve shape and tone, and strengthen the body for both women and men.

Due to the lack of the male hormone testosterone, women are not likely to develop bulging muscles without using anabolic steroids—which are illegal and especially harmful to women.

Not only can women use all parts of this book to become fit, but in so doing, they will look better and feel better. However, there are some differences between the sexes that will help women become better able to pursue their exercises.

Cardiovascular conditioning (working of your heart and vascular system) results in equal benefits for women and for men. In skeletal training, however, there are big differences primarily due to hormonal differences. Both men and women secrete the male sex hormone testosterone and the female sex hormone estrogen. There are differences because men have a higher level of testosterone than women and women have a higher level of estrogen than men circulating throughout their bodies.

Testosterone, along with weight training, increases muscle mass (hypertrophy). Therefore, women rarely experience dramatic changes in muscular development from weight training (unless they have an unusually high level of testosterone or use anabolic steroids). This is why no matter how hard or often they train, they will not wind up looking like Mr. America.

Men and women have somewhat different bone structures. The woman's pelvic girdle is wider than that of a man's, which helps her in childbirth. However, women's knees are the same distance apart as men's. Thus, women place more stress on their knees than men. Thus, women are more likely to develop knee problems performing exercises that cause stress to their knees, such as deep squats.

Most women do not have a problem with exercising. However, some women who train exceptionally hard for long periods of time sometimes will cease menstruation. The medical term for this is *amenorrhea*. Research indicates that low body fat (8 to 10 percent) and a combination of heavy training and/or mental stress can cause this condition. If a woman wants to reverse this condition, she needs to cut back on her training, try to reduce her mental stress, and raise her body fat to a level above 10 percent.

Women who are physically fit generally have fewer problems and shorter and easier labor during pregnancy. Pregnant women should check with their doctor before beginning an exercise program. Most doctors agree that exercise during pregnancy will provide a better cardiovascular condition, better muscle tone, a reduction in tension, and a higher level of endurance. Yet, it is better to be fit prior to pregnancy and not suddenly begin a strenuous fitness program after conception. During pregnancy, women should avoid extreme exertion and overheating and must immediately stop all exercise if they feel faint. Remember, if you are pregnant or thinking about having a child, you must consult your physician prior to starting any new exercise program!

The American Dietetic Association (2000) states that "recent evidence suggests that lactating women who exercise have significantly lower body fat and higher energy expenditures than nonexercising women. In addition, exercising women produce a slightly greater volume of milk. Lactating women who exercise should consume sufficient fluids to avoid dehydration and sufficient energy to compensate for that expended during exercise."

Women, naturally, have a higher percentage of body fat than men. This is true in the general population where the ideal body fat percentage for men is 14 to 18 percent and for women it is 18 to 24 percent. Among male athletes, this ratio is 4 to 10 percent, and for female athletes it is 10 to 14 percent. Exercise can reduce body fat for both sexes. Body fat levels "greater than 26 percent for men and 29 percent for women are considered a potential risk factor for the development of chronic diseases," according to the American Dietetic Association (2000).

Quick weight loss programs result in a loss of muscle tissue. It is not the way to achieve total fitness. Since women have less muscle mass, extreme diet programs are more damaging to the female physique than to the male. When women cut back on their food intake enough to reduce inches around their thighs and hips, their upper bodies also are affected. A loss of two pounds per week results in a loss of muscle size.

With weight training and exercise and the muscle they develop, women can achieve muscular balance and harmonious body proportions.

Women burn fat optimally about twenty minutes into exercise and stop burning fat sooner than men about an hour after exercise. Men may start burning fat as soon as they begin exercising and continue for hours after exercising. Intense short-burst activities such as tennis or strength training cause the body to release a chemical, noradrenaline, which is a powerful fat burner which causes the body to use more fat for energy following the workout.

Weight training and conditioning are the fastest and easiest ways to improve the shape, tone, and strength of a woman's body. Running, swimming, cycling, and taking aerobics classes are excellent cardiovascular conditioners to burn calories, but they cannot compare with the increase of strength and lean body mass that result from weight training.

When a woman starts a weight training program and stays with it, she will notice many changes in a few weeks. Even if a woman does not lose any weight, she will discover that many clothes that she could not fit into suddenly fit once again. This is true because muscle weighs more than fat. As a woman gains muscle and burns fat, her mirror and clothes will indicate more to her than her bathroom scales.

As a woman's abdominal muscles become stronger, her stomach becomes flatter. "Flabby" areas of the body may become firmer: the triceps (the back of the upper arms will tighten up) and the fatty deposits on the thighs and buttocks may diminish and gradually will be replaced by firm, toned muscles. Small breasted women often notice an increase in bust size while women with large breasts will notice their breasts becoming firmer and sagging less.

As with men, women often give up weight training shortly after beginning it. Here is why! When a woman performs two sets of twenty to thirty repetitions for each exercise in her routine and does not significantly improve the shape of her body, she might feel that training is useless and a waste of time. Or if she lost ten to fifteen pounds of body weight while jogging or dieting, the low-weight/high-repetition routine will not help her to get rid of her flabbiness. This is because she simply cannot build muscle or tone her body, to any real degree, by doing too many repetitions with too little weight. She must remember that building and toning takes place when the muscles are challenged by heavy resistance.

The Effects of Weight Training on the Aging Process

What is the effect of weight training on the aging process? The longer we live, the more gravity pulls on our bodies, causing the spine to compress and the muscles to sag. We burn fewer calories as we get older, so we tend to put on fat, and this puts more of a strain on our system. Older people are generally more sedentary than younger ones. This results in poor cardiovascular conditioning and muscular atrophy.

Ironically, much of what we think of as aging has nothing to do with aging itself. It is simply deterioration. When we say that someone looks thirty, forty, or fifty years old, we are saying that this person looks the way we expect someone to look at that age. However, if you look closely at many dedicated weight lifters, you will not see any double chins, sagging jowls and pectorals, or flabby stomachs. Those who have kept up their training simply do not fit into our expectations. It is hard to judge just how old they are.

Weight training slows or even reverses some of the most insidious effects of aging. Aging is bound to catch up with us all sooner or later. But later is better. When people ask if they are too old to weight train, the answer is that they are never too old not to begin weight training.

The older you get, the more important it is for you to train and become physically fit. It is also true that the older you are, the more amazed you will be at what a total fitness program, including weight training, can do for you, your life, your looks, your health, your personal safety on the job, and your personal relationships with others on and off the job. As people age, their bones become more brittle and vulnerable to breaking. By performing training exercises, you can help prevent this.

Osteoporosis is a major health concern for both men and women, but it is an especially critical factor among women. According to the American Dietetic Association, osteoporosis "is related to calcium intake, estrogen level, alcohol and caffeine intake, family history, and the amount and type of physical activity . . . . Achieving a recommended daily intake of calcium in conjunction with performing regular weight-bearing activities, will promote the deposition of calcium in bone and thereby reduce the risk of developing osteoporosis." Weight training can help to delay the onset of osteoporosis and/or stop its spread.

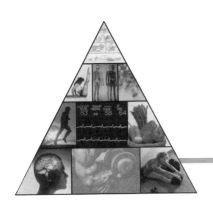

How Often Should I Weight Train?

You probably are asking yourself, "How do I get started?" and "How often should I exercise?" The general rule is that you should try to weight train at least three times per week, about thirty to sixty minutes per session, with a rest day following each workout. You will get your best results when you apply stress to your body in a hard day/easy day sequence. This allows for cellular changes to occur on your rest days. This also allows for your muscles to recover from the stress of your workout and automatically rebuild stronger. Therefore, to begin your training cycle, you should workout on a Monday, Wednesday, Friday or Tuesday, Thursday, Saturday sequence. Never skip a rest day! It is just as important to rest (recover) as it is to exercise. The Surgeon General recommends exercising five to seven times per week for thirty minutes each time.

What are Sets and Repetitions?

When you exercise, you perform sets and repetitions for each exercise. A set is a fixed number of repetitions (reps), or repeated movements of an exercise. Although there are many options to the number of sets, functional strength gains will come from one to three sets per exercise. To start out your program, you will need to stick to ten repetitions per exercise (except for your stomach).

How Much Weight Should I Lift?

How much weight is suitable at the start? A good rule of thumb is to use as much weight as you are comfortable with to perform ten repetitions. The last repetition should be fairly difficult to perform. You should use the first few exercise sessions primarily as testing sessions to determine how much weight you can handle safely. Once you are able to perform more than fifteen repetitions, you should increase the amount of weight you use.

What Are the Types of Lifting Programs?

There are two different basic types of lifting programs. They each produce different results. One is designed for strength and the other is for endurance. If you want to gain strength, you will need to perform low repetitions with heavier weights. However, if you want to gain muscular endurance, then you will want to perform your exercises with high repetitions with less weight. When you want to develop muscular endurance, or the ability of your muscles to produce force repeatedly over a specified period of time, you will need to train with lighter weights and higher repetitions. This also produces the "pump" effect, an increase in blood flow to the muscle group being worked.

There are seven basic muscle groups in your body. In each of the beginning exercise sessions, you will need to work all seven groups. The larger muscle groups need to be worked before the smaller ones. Why? If you fatigue the smaller muscle groups first, you cannot work the larger groups adequately. For example, if you work your biceps first, you fatigue your arms (small group). Then, when you exercise your chest and back, (large groups), you limit yourself because you cannot adequately exercise your chest muscles, due to your fatigued arm muscles.

What Order of Exercises Should I Follow?

A typical order of exercises includes the following:
- Abdominal (stomach). Begin with this muscle group and use it as a partial warm-up.
- Back. Be sure that you are thoroughly warmed up before working this large muscle group.
- Thighs (legs and rear end). Since the legs automatically bring the muscles of the lower back into play, make sure that you are thoroughly warmed up prior to working your thighs. This is the largest muscle group in your body.
- Chest
- Shoulders
- Triceps
- Biceps. Work the biceps and triceps last because they are the smallest of the muscle groups.

What is Cardiovascular Training?

Your cardiovascular/respiratory training is an important component of your general conditioning program. It refers to exercises that strengthen your heart, lungs, and respiratory system. You may receive your cardiovascular training in your local gym, by moving rapidly through your workout routine from one exercise to another. However, it is more efficient to run, jog, swim, cycle (stationary/tour), hike, or walk briskly. You should try to do some type of cardiovascular activity for at least thirty minutes, five to seven times per week, according to the Surgeon General's Report on Physical Activity (1994). A good time is a day when you are not weight training.

What Guidelines Should I Follow?

Remember, exercise alone will not provide fitness or build muscle mass. Other factors such as proper diet, sleep and rest, and the quality of life also matter. You will need to weight train three nonconsecutive days per week. For example, Monday, Wednesday, Friday or Tuesday, Thursday, Saturday. You will need to exercise consistently three days per week for approximately the first three months. Following this period, you can increase your workout sessions to four or five times weekly or try three consecutive workout sessions and rest for one day and continue to follow the same routine pattern until you wish to try something new. However, consistency in training is always the major key to fitness success. To obtain the best results in your exercise programs, you must try to:

- Get plenty of rest and sleep.
- At the start, consistently exercise three nonconsecutive days weekly
- Exercise on alternate days.
- Arrange your daily schedule so that you can exercise at the same time each day.
- Eat good quality, properly prepared foods high in vitamins, minerals, and complex carbohydrates (see Chapter 3).
- Drink plenty of water—at least eight to ten sixteen-ounce glasses each day.
- Maintain a positive attitude and believe in yourself.

Can I Exercise at Home?

Since you have purchased this exercise program, you may have decided to perform your workout sessions at home. A home gym offers privacy and a chance to exercise at times that are convenient for you. You can build your own home gym from the ground up. At the beginning, you will need to purchase an adjustable barbell and dumbbell set, an adjustable incline exercise bench, and a pair of squat stands. Later, you can add other pieces of equipment as you advance in the program.

Some excellent home gyms are available. Some are much more expensive than others for those who desire to train at home with more sophisticated equipment than just free weights and a bench. Some complete exercise machines can cost thousands of dollars, while other exercise machines on the market are less complicated and expensive, but may still cost around $600.

This may seem like a large outlay of cash. However, home gym equipment is a one-time expenditure. Look at it this way, if you decide at some point to exercise in a commercial gym, you must pay dues on a monthly or annual basis. Or, even though you perform most of your exercise sessions at a public gym, you still will find that a home gym is much more convenient.

To begin with, all you really need to get started in your workout routine is a barbell and dumbbell set. This consists of a long bar (barbell) and two shorter bars (dumbbells) and a number of individual weight "plates" that fit together on any of the bars. You can find a 110 pound set of weights in most sporting goods stores for as little as $40.00. Some weight sets have plastic plates filled with sand, and others have plates made of iron. Either kind are suitable. However, plastic plates do have an advantage because they will not scratch the floor.

There are only two considerations when choosing a weight set:

- The weights must be interchangeable. Progressive resistance training requires that you add weight to the bar as you become stronger. Solid dumbbells, to which weight cannot be added, will not allow you to take advantage of the adaptation of muscle to progressively greater stress. If you do decide to purchase solid dumbbells, you will need to purchase the entire set—and that can get expensive.
- Your weight set must include two-and-a-half-pound plates. However, you should be careful with your purchase because some weight sets come with no plates smaller than five pounds. Since you add weight by placing a plate on both ends of the bar, then the smallest addition you could make to the bar would be ten pounds. This additional amount could be just too much of a jump. Two-and-a-half-pound plates allow for a more convenient five-pound weight increase.

In addition to the weights and bars, you will need to purchase an adjustable exercise bench with a rack and an attachment that will allow you to perform leg exercises. Some benches can be very expensive. However, they can be purchased for less than a hundred dollars. Just be sure that the one you choose is safe and sturdy enough to stand up to your weight lifting needs.

Another basic piece of equipment that you might want to purchase is a chinning bar. Without using some fairly complex exercise machines, the chinning bar is one way to develop back strength. Adjustable bars that fit in most doorways are also available in most sporting goods stores.

You also might consider purchasing an abdominal slant board to help you firm up and develop your waistline and stomach. Be sure that you try out the board prior to taking it home because it could be too flimsy and totally unsafe. There is a lot of difference between a 100-pound woman using a piece of equipment and subjecting it to the forces generated by an active 200-pound man.

Many equipment manufacturers are trying to "make a buck" on the exercise and fitness craze with devices, springs and levers, and chrome "doodads" that are supposed to help you get into shape. If you are really serious about fitness, these things are, generally, a waste of your money. Save your money for some piece of equipment that really will help you train.

If you have access to a gym, you can train there following this program. But if you want to work out at home, all you need is this program, the basic equipment we have discussed, and enough room to train safely.

Enough room is extremely important. Even if you have enough clearance to work with your weights, you need to feel that you will not bang your equipment into things around your workout area. This can distract you and seriously interfere with your concentration. Try exercising in your living room, bedroom, garage, basement, or in your back yard. Train wherever you feel most comfortable.

Some other things that you might try include some degree of privacy (family members parading through your workout area can break your concentration as well). Have enough light to see with and choose a well-ventilated room.

When Should I Exercise?

Remember, digestion takes blood and so does heavy exercise. Therefore, to have enough blood available to feed your muscles, avoid performing strenuous exercise while your stomach is full. Protein and fat take a long time to digest. Therefore, wait quite a long time after eating steak before you train. Salads and vegetables take less time to pass through the stomach so you do not have to wait as long. Fruits digest very quickly, and the fructose (sugar) it contains converts easily to glucose to produce energy for exercise. Hence, you can eat moderate amounts of fruit just before and even during your workout sessions.

Picking a time to exercise that fits conveniently into your daily schedule is very important. Some individuals like to train by 6:00 A.M. By 8:00 A.M. they have trained, showered, eaten breakfast, and are ready to face the day.

Some people hardly can wake up first thing in the morning, much less do a workout routine. If that is your case, you might find that it is much more convenient for you to train after you get home from work and before dinner.

Some staff workout during their lunch hour and prefer to do their training then. They skip eating lunch all together. Again, that is a matter of personal choice and circumstances.

Why Should I Vary My Exercise Regimen?

Your body gets used to moving in certain ways. By trying new and different exercises for each body muscle group, you can add to your flexibility and hit the muscles in a slightly different way. Learn the exercises in this book first for the schedules given, then you can try other exercises. Besides, fresh exercises break the monotony. For example, you can mix both machines and free weights.

What is a Split System?

There is another type of training referred to as the "split system" that involves exercising different parts of your body during separate workouts. This is helpful for those people who cannot dedicate a long period of time, all in one session, to training but still want to get a full workout or for those who want to weight train every day. By splitting the body parts (for example, upper body/lower body), the muscles still get the required "day off" but you can train every day.

Why is Proper Technique Important?

A proper technique of lifting will improve performance, minimize workout time, speed up improvement, and help prevent injuries.

Why is Stretching a Part of this Program?

Stretching before lifting prepares the joints for motion, extends the range of motion of the muscles, and helps avoid injuries. Stretching after your workout slowly takes the stress off the muscles and helps you to wind down from your routine, relaxes you, and helps to reduce soreness. If you exercise through the whole range of motion of the joints, you will maintain and possibly improve your flexibility. Testing has demonstrated that top weight lifters are among the most flexible athletes. (*See* Chapter 9 on Stretching.)

What is a Warm Up?

Warming up prepares your joints and muscles for activity. Often, lifters will perform a light set of lifts for warming up. This brings the blood to the specific muscles to be worked. Some others warm up by doing pushups, sit-ups, light calisthenics, jogging, or by using a stationary bike. If the weather is cold or if you are sore from previous workout routines, you especially need to make sure that you warm up thoroughly. (*See* Chapter 9 on Stretching.)

What is a Proper Stance?

When you are lifting weights from a standing position, be sure your feet are at least a little wider than shoulder width apart. This balances you. Some lifters wear training foot gear with heels to help offset the shifting of their center of gravity when lifting heavy weights. Or at times, a two-inch by four-inch board is placed under their heels when they are performing exercises, such as squats, to help them maintain their balance.

Always maintain proper spinal alignment. Proper spinal alignment means that your neck is aligned with your spine and you should have an imaginary straight line that connects your ears to your shoulder, shoulders to the hip, hip to the knee and knee to the heel.

What is Meant by Proper Breathing?

Proper breathing technique is extremely important when doing any exercise. Never hold your breath when you are lifting. It can stop the flow of oxygen to your brain and cause you to pass out. This can be extremely dangerous—especially if you are lifting heavy weights. Try to breathe in and out through both your nose and mouth. By breathing only through your nose, you may not receive enough oxygen.

Try to breathe out during the exertion (it may be a push phase or a pull phase) and breathe in as you return the weight to the start position. Breath control during the lift is extremely important and, for your safety, you must have it. While performing a bench press, for example, inhale as you lower the weight to your chest, and exhale as you press the bar back to its starting position.

What Should I Know to Be Safe When Lifting Weights?

While you lift, you should be concerned about your safety at all times. The following are some safety tips that you should observe for your personal safety:

- Try not to train alone. Even if you own a home gym, try to have someone there to assist you if you need it. Most serious weight training injuries occur when the lifter is training alone.
- Always have a "spotter" for your most difficult lifts, such as, for bench presses and squats when you approach your strength limits. Serious accidents have occurred when lifters have been pinned by the weight doing bench presses.
- Use safety collars on barbells. If you do not, the weights could slip off the end, causing the other end to quickly move downward toward the floor, throwing you off balance and possibly injuring your back or other joints or muscles.
- Use the proper position for all exercises. Study the positions for each exercise in this book.

You must be especially careful not to only exercise "showy" muscle groups, such as your arms, chest, and shoulders. Many beginners are eager to overexercise these muscle groups because they are easy to show off to others. This is not wise. Never neglect any body part. The body needs harmony to truly work well. This means that it is vital to exercise your abdomen, legs, and back, as well.

What If I Miss a Regular Workout?

Always try to make each and every workout. However, a lot of things can happen to interfere with a scheduled workout. When something interferes with your working out, there is no use in becoming upset about it. The trick is to do something every day, even if it only involves taking a walk or doing some sit-ups and calisthenics. For those times when you are away from home or the gym and cannot follow your regular weight training routine, there are some substitute exercise routines in this book that are very useful. If you miss a week or more of workouts, then workout at a lower level so that you do not injure yourself. Build up again to where you were. This is particularly important if you were out due to illness.

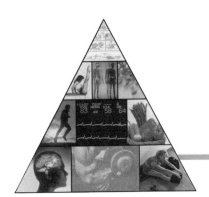

CHAPTER 6:

The Variable Cyclic Phase System

One of the primary reasons for writing this book for corrections and law enforcement professionals is to make suggestions and recommendations on fitness programs that will work. Due to strange, rotating shift schedules, many times officers feel that they do not have time to exercise. With other family and personal commitments, it is difficult to find time to work out. Yet, if you could learn that you do not need to spend lots of money on equipment to work out your entire body, would you try that? Or, if you could work out safely and spend only thirty to forty-five minutes per workout session, three to four times weekly to maintain your fitness level, would you believe that? If you follow this program, you can have it all!

Five Phases to Fitness

Essential Components of a Well-planned and Well-balanced Fitness Program

- Overload—To get the benefits of exercise, you must put stress on a muscle beyond what you have done previously. If you keep doing what you always have done, you will get the same results you always have or even worse, you will be able to do less.
- Progression—You start with lighter weights and work up to heavier weights lifted more times. Start out slowly and add weights, repetitions, or extra time for activity in small increments.
- Balance—This means weight training should be combined with aerobic activity, flexibility, and stretching. Weights by themselves are not the whole answer to being fit and in shape no more than protein alone is the sole answer to a diet.

Weight training is the core of this program, but all other aspects of systematic training techniques, for example, aerobics and flexibility, are also very important. Before you start your weight training session each day, you need to set aside some time to warm up and stretch without rushing. Once you have become loose and relaxed (warmed up), then begin your training routine. Your warm up is literally that. It should be sufficient to raise your body temperature one to two degrees. After you have completed your session and are ready to put your weights away, take time to cool down. This will counteract any shortening of your muscles, tendons, and ligaments that can be brought on by weight training. At the end of your session, you may wish to do some additional stretches to cool down and to rid your body of lactic acid buildup that leads to soreness. A hot shower after exercising or a warm bath the evening after exercising also helps to reduce soreness.

The Variable Cyclic Phase System consists of five five-week phases. Each phase builds on the other. Phase one (the preparatory phase) consists of fifteen workout sessions (three workout sessions per week for five weeks) of specially arranged exercises. A list of exercises for this phase begin on page 51. Phase two (the intermediate phase) helps you to increase the number of workout sessions. It consists of twenty workout sessions (four workout sessions per week for five weeks). Phase three (the conditioning phase) increases the number of exercise sessions. It includes twenty-five workout routines (five workout sessions per week for five weeks). Phase four (the power phase) creates additional strength and power in your lifts and involves twenty-five workout sessions (five workout sessions per week for five weeks). And lastly, Phase five (the maintenance phase) helps you to maintain your conditioning level. Then, following a week when you lay off after Phase five, you return to Phase three (the conditioning phase) and start the program from Phase three and proceed to Phase five but with your new levels of strength, power, and endurance. Good luck with your program.

This is your book. On any of the exercises, write your comments that will help you the next time. You might want to indicate your settings on any machine, the weight level you use, or any other notation that will aid you. On page 169 is your exercise journal. Use it to keep track of your progress.

While you are doing the exercise, try to visualize what is happening to your muscles. Refer to the pictures of the muscles in Figures 6.1 and 6.2 on pages 49-50. Then, when you have some free time, attempt to go through the exercises in your head. This creative visualization will enable you to do the exercises with greater confidence and move ahead in the program.

Before you begin this or any other exercise program, it is important that you check in with your doctor. This is especially vital if you have been sedentary for some time or if you have some physical problems or problems for which you are taking medications. It is particularly important to check with your doctor if you are pregnant and are just beginning an exercise program. Exercise can have an impact on the dosage of your medication and your overall health. Certain exercises may have an adverse impact on your body due to previous problems so your doctor can suggest what types of things to avoid or perhaps what to substitute.

The exercises are arranged according to body part—working from the larger groups to the smaller. Generally, you should do the exercises that are recommended in each

Figure 6.1: Anterior View of Major Muscles

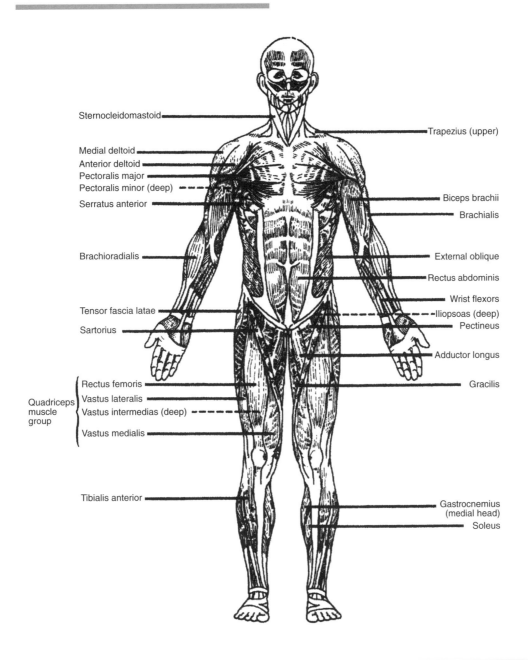

Sternocleidomastoid

Medial deltoid
Anterior deltoid
Pectoralis major
Pectoralis minor (deep)
Serratus anterior

Brachioradialis

Tensor fascia latae

Sartorius

Quadriceps
muscle
group
{
Rectus femoris
Vastus lateralis
Vastus intermedias (deep)
Vastus medialis
}

Tibialis anterior

Trapezius (upper)

Biceps brachii
Brachialis

External oblique
Rectus abdominis
Wrist flexors
Iliopsoas (deep)
Pectineus

Adductor longus

Gracilis

Gastrocnemius
(medial head)
Soleus

Courtesy of National Strength Professionals Association, Gaithersburg, Maryland.

segment, but after you get proficient in them, you can alternate with other exercises that work the same muscle group. Certainly, if your doctor makes recommendations about types of exercises, follow the doctor's recommendations rather than the guidelines in this book.

Note: If the number of sets is not listed, simply count the\marks as in 6\8\10 to mean that you perform three sets and on the first you do six repetitions, on the second

Figure 6.2: Posterior View of Major Muscles

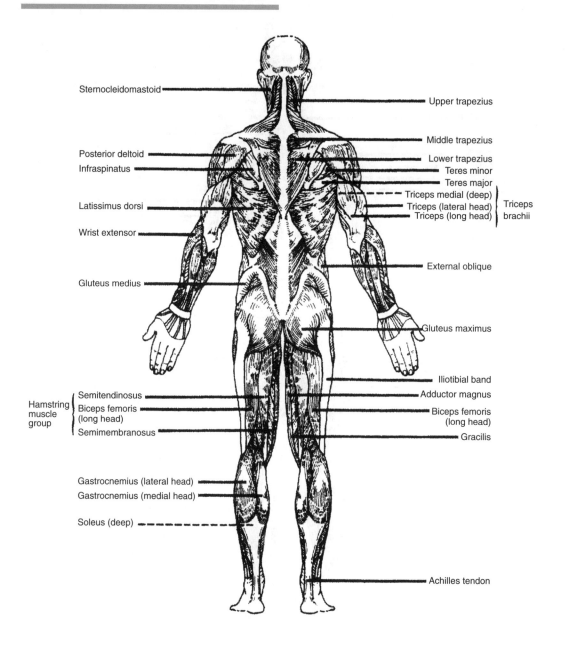

Sternocleidomastoid — Upper trapezius

Middle trapezius

Posterior deltoid — Lower trapezius
Infraspinatus — Teres minor
Teres major
Triceps medial (deep)
Latissimus dorsi — Triceps (lateral head) } Triceps brachii
Triceps (long head)

Wrist extensor

External oblique

Gluteus medius

Gluteus maximus

Iliotibial band

Hamstring muscle group { Semitendinosus — Adductor magnus
Biceps femoris (long head) — Biceps femoris (long head)
Semimembranosus — Gracilis

Gastrocnemius (lateral head)
Gastrocnemius (medial head)

Soleus (deep)

Achilles tendon

Courtesy of National Strength Professionals Association, Gaithersburg, Maryland.

you do eight repetitions, and on the third you do ten repetitions. The word *each* means that you do each side, for example, on the side leg lift you do two sets and lift each leg ten times during each set, or forty lifts altogether.

The rest period is the time between the sets of each exercise.

Phase One—The Preparatory Phase

Muscle Group	Exercise	Sets/ Reps	Rest Period	Page
Abdomen	Crunch–Front	2 x 15	1 min.	104
Abdomen	Leg Kick–Alternate	2 x 10 ea.	1 min.	106
Abdomen	Leg Lift	2 x 10 ea.	1 min.	107
Abdomen	Side Bender with Dumbbells	2 x 15	1 min.	109
Chest	Bench Press on Incline	2 x 8/10	1 min.	113
Chest	Fly on Flat Bench with Dumbbells	2 x 8/10	1 min.	116
Back	Row, Bent-over with Dumbbells or Barbell	2 x 8/10	1 min.	130
Back	Fly-Back, Lying	2 x 8/10	1 min.	144
Thighs	Lunge, Front	2 x 8/10 ea.	1 min.	140
Thighs	Squat	2 x 10	1 min.	141
Shoulders	Press, Seated Dumbbell	2 x 8/10	1 min.	146
Shoulders	Shoulder Shrug with Dumbbell	2 x 8/10 ea.*	1 min.	150
Triceps	Tricep Extension	2 x 8	1 min.	155
Triceps	Tricep Extension, One-Handed Dumbbell	2 x 8/10 ea.*	1 min.	156
Biceps	Curl, Seated Close Grip Concentration Barbell	2 x 8/10	1 min.	159
Biceps	Curl, Seated Alternating Dumbbell	2 x 8/10	1 min.	158

Note: 2 x 8/10 each means do two sets of eight on each leg and then do two sets of ten on each leg.

Things to Remember:

By weight training once per week, you can maintain a "reasonable" level of fitness. If you weight train twice per week, you can make some physical improvement. Training three times per week is recommended. With this option, you can see noticeable improvement. Train on either Monday, Wednesday, Friday OR Tuesday, Thursday, Saturday. Note: time is not important, though sessions probably will last twenty to sixty minutes. However, if you only can exercise for a shorter time on a particular day, do not forego the exercise time as this will break your habit. A rest day between each day of exercise will help your muscles to heal.

Use as much weight as is comfortable, yet challenging, to do the number of repetitions you are shown. If you start off to high, you may get discouraged and not return. Try a low level of weight and build up gradually. Otherwise you are apt to hurt yourself or become frustrated and quit. If it takes you longer than the suggested regimen, this is okay. Increase the weight you use once the sets and repetitions become easy. Your last repetition should feel difficult. Do not be discouraged if you cannot do all the repetitions listed. Do as many of them as you are able to do. Eventually, you will be able to do the number indicated. It is okay if it takes you longer to achieve the goals in each section than the suggested time frame. The important thing is to give yourself credit for doing something. Your persistence will pay off. Some exercises will be easier than others. This is normal for everyone.

Exhale on the exertion or first phase and inhale on the return. Be sure you are not holding your breath.

If you feel any pain, STOP! Find another exercise that works the same muscle group, but that causes no pain.

Phase Two—The Intermediate Phase

Muscle Group	Exercise	Sets/ Reps	Rest Period	Page
Abdomen	Sit-up on Decline	3 x 15	1 min.	110
Abdomen	Leg Lift	3 x 15	1 min.	107
Chest	Overhead Press on Machine	3 x 8/10	1 min.	145
Chest	Fly on Flat Bench with Dumbbells	3 x 8/10	1 min.	116
Back	Lower Back Stretch	3 x 15	1 min.	127
Back	Cable Row	3 x 8/10	1 min.	122
Back	Row, Bent-over with Dumbbells or Barbell	3 x 8/10	1 min.	130
Legs	Squat	3 x 8/10	1 min.	141
Legs	Leg Extension	3 x 8/10	1 min.	137
Shoulders	Press, Seated Dumbbell	3 x 8/10	1 min.	146
Shoulders	Raise, Seated Side Lateral	3 x 8/10	1 min.	148
Triceps	Kickback	3 x 8/10	1 min.	153
Triceps	Cable Push Down on Machine	3 x 8/10	1 min.	151
Biceps	Preacher Curl	3 x 8/10	1 min.	161
Biceps	Curl, Seated Dumbbell	3 x 8/10	1 min.	160

Things to Remember:

For best results, in this phase, train four times per week. Exercise your abdominals on four days and your chest, back, and legs on two nonconsecutive days. Exercise your shoulders, triceps, and biceps on two other nonconsecutive days. Try to complete your exercise sessions in forty-five to sixty minutes each day.

Use as much weight as is comfortable for the number of repetitions shown. Your last repetitions should feel difficult. Once your sets and repetitions become fairly easy, increase the amount of weight so that the last repetition is again difficult. Exhale on the exertion–the first phase–and inhale on the return. By this time, you should be more conscious of how your breathing has an impact on your ability to exercise.

If you feel any pain whatsoever, STOP! Find another exercise that works the same muscle group, but one that causes no pain.

Phase Three—The Conditioning Phase

Week one of the Conditioning Phase

Muscle Group	Exercise	Sets/ Reps	Rest Period	Page
Week one: Monday of the Conditioning Phase				
Abdomen	Sit-up on Decline	3 x 15	1 min.	110
Abdomen	Sit-up, V	3 x 15 ea.	1 min.	111
Abdomen	Leg Lift	3 x 12/15	1 min.	107
Back	Pull, Seated Two Arm Low Lat	12/10/8	1 min./ set	129
Back	Pull, Reverse Grip	10/8/6	1 min./ set	128
Legs	Squat	10/8/6	1 min./ set	141
Legs	Leg Extension on Leg Machine	12/10/8	1 min./ set	137
Legs	Hamstring Curl	12/10/8	1 min./ set	135
Calves	Calf Raise	3 x 15	1 min./ set	133
Week one: Tuesday of the Conditioning Phase				
Abdomen	Crunch-Front	3 x 20	1 min./ set	104
Abdomen	Side Bender with Dumbbells	3 x 10 ea.	1 min./ set	109
Abdomen	Leg Kick-Alternate	3 x 20	1 min./ set	106
Chest	Overhead Press on Machine	10/8/6	1 min./ set	145
Chest	Fly on Flat Bench with Dumbbells	12/10/8	1 min./ set	116
Shoulders	Press, Seated Dumbbell	10/8/6	1 min./ set	146
Shoulders	Raise, Seated Side Lateral	12/10/8	1 min./ set	148
Shoulders	Bent Over Raise	10/8/6	1 min./ set	143
Forearms	Curl, Front Wrist	15/12/10	1 min./ set	162
Week one: Wednesday of the Conditioning Phase				
Abdomen	Crunch-Open Leg	3 x 20	1 min./ set	105
Abdomen	Side Bender with Dumbbells	3 x 15 ea.	1 min./ set	109
Abdomen	Rear Flutter Kick	3 x 10	1 min./ set	108
Triceps	Tricep Extension	12/10/8	1 min./ set	155
Triceps	Cable Push Down on Machine	10/8/6	1 min./ set	151
Biceps	Curl, Seated Close Grip Concentration Barbell	10/8/6	1 min./ set	159
Biceps	Curl Seated Dumbbell	12/10/8	1 min./ set	160
Forearms	Curl, Reverse Grip Wrist	15/12/10	1 min./ set	164

Week one: Thursday of the Conditioning Phase

Abdomen	Sit-up, V	3 x 20	1 min./ set	111
Abdomen	Leg Lift	3 x 15	1 min./ set	107
Abdomen	Rear Flutter Kick	3 x 20	1 min./ set	108
Legs	Squat	10/8/6	1 min./ set	141
Legs	Leg Extension on Leg Machine	12/10/8	1 min./ set	137
Legs	Hamstring Curl	10/8/6	1 min./ set	135
Back	Row, Upright	10/8/6	1 min./ set	149
Back	Pull, Reverse Grip	12/10/8	1 min./ set	128
Calves	Calf Raise	15/12/10	1 min./ set	133

Week one: Friday of the Conditioning Phase

Abdomen	Crunch-Front	3 x 20	1 min./ set	104
Abdomen	Side Bender with Dumbbells	3 x 10 ea.	1 min./ set	109
Abdomen	Leg Kick-Alternate	3 x 20	1 min./ set	106
Chest	Bench Press on Incline with Barbell	12/10/8	1 min./ set	114
Chest	Fly on Flat Bench with Dumbbells	12/10/8	1 min./ set	116
Shoulders	Press, Seated Dumbbell	12/10/8	1 min./ set	146
Shoulders	Row, Upright	10/8/6	1 min./ set	149
Triceps	Kickback	10/8/6	1 min./ set	153
Triceps	Tricep Extension, One-handed Dumbbell	12/10/8	1 min./ set	156

Week two of the Conditioning Phase

Muscle Group	Exercise	Sets/ Reps	Rest Period	Page
Week two: Monday of the Conditioning Phase				
Abdomen	Sit-up on Decline	3 x 15	1 min.	110
Abdomen	Sit-up, V	3 x 15 ea.	1 min.	111
Abdomen	Leg Lift	3 x 12/15	1 min.	107
Legs	Squat with Barbell	10/8/6	1 min./ set	142
Legs	Hamstring Curl	12/10/8	1 min./ set	135
Calves	Calf Raise Seated with Barbell	3 x 20	1 min./ set	134
Calves	Calf Machine	3 x 15	1 min./ set	132
Biceps	Preacher Curl	12/10/8	1 min./ set	161
Biceps	Curl, Seated Dumbbell	12/10/8	1 min./ set	160

Week two: Tuesday of the Conditioning Phase

Abdomen	Sit-up, V	3 x 20	1 min./ set	111
Abdomen	Side Bender with Dumbbells	3 x 10 ea.	1 min./ set	109
Abdomen	Leg Kick-Alternate	3 x 20	1 min./ set	106
Back	Row, Bent-over with Dumbbells or Barbell	12/10/8 ea.	1 min./ set	130
Back	Pull, Seated Two Arm Low Lat	10/8/6	1 min./ set	129
Chest	Bench Press on Incline	10/8/6	1 min./ set	113
Chest	Fly on Flat Bench with Dumbbells	12/10/8	1 min./ set	116
Shoulders	Raise, Seated Side Lateral	12/10/8	1 min./ set	148
Shoulders	Row, Upright	10/8/6	1 min./ set	149

Week two: Wednesday of the Conditioning Phase

Abdomen	Sit-up, V	3 x 20	1 min./ set	111
Abdomen	Side Bender with Dumbbells	3 x 15 ea.	1 min./ set	109
Abdomen	Rear Flutter Kick	3 x 10	1 min./ set	108
Biceps	Curl, Seated Alternating Dumbbell	10/8/6	1 min./ set	158
Biceps	Curl, Seated Close Grip Concentration Barbell	12/10/8	1 min./ set	159
Triceps	Tricep Close Grip Bench Press	10/8/6	1 min./ set	154
Triceps	Tricep Extension, One-handed Dumbbell	12/10/8	1 min./ set	156
Forearms	Curl, Front Wrist	15/12/10	1 min./ set	162
Forearms	Curl, Reverse Grip Wrist	15/12/10	1 min./ set	164

Week two: Thursday of the Conditioning Phase

Abdomen	Sit-up on Decline	3 x 20	1 min./ set	110
Abdomen	Leg Lift	3 x 15	1 min./ set	107
Abdomen	Rear Flutter Kick	3 x 20	1 min./ set	108
Legs	Squat with Barbell	10/8/6	1 min./ set	142
Legs	Leg Extension on Leg Machine	12/10/8	1 min./ set	137
Legs	Squat	10/8/6	1 min./ set	141
Back	Lateral Pull, Close Grip Front	10/8/6	1 min./ set	126
Back	Row, Bent-over with Dumbbells or Barbell	12/10/8	1 min./ set	130
Calves	Calf Raise	15/12/10	1 min./ set	133

Week two: Friday of the Conditioning Phase

Abdomen	Sit-up, V	3 x 20	1 min./ set	111
Abdomen	Leg Lift	3 x 15	1 min./ set	107
Abdomen	Leg Kick-Alternate	3 x 20	1 min./ set	106

Muscle Group	Exercise	Sets/Reps	Rest Period	Page
Chest	Bench Press on Incline	12/10/8	1 min./ set	113
Chest	Fly on Flat Bench with Dumbbells	12/10/8	1 min./ set	116
Shoulders	Press, Seated Dumbbell	12/10/8	1 min./ set	146
Shoulders	Row, Upright	10/8/6	1 min./ set	149
Triceps	Tricep Extension	12/10/8	1 min./ set	155
Triceps	Cable Push Down on Machine	10/8/6	1 min./ set	151

Week three of the Conditioning Phase

Muscle Group	Exercise	Sets/Reps	Rest Period	Page
Week three: Monday of the Conditioning Phase				
Abdomen	Sit-up on Decline	3 x 15	1 min.	110
Abdomen	Sit-up, V	3 x 15 ea.	1 min.	111
Abdomen	Leg Lift	3 x 12/15	1 min.	107
Legs	Squat	10/8/6	1 min./ set	141
Legs	Leg Extension on Leg Machine	12/10/8	1 min./ set	137
Legs	Hamstring Curl	10/8/6	1 min./ set	135
Biceps	Preacher Curl	12/10/8	1 min./ set	161
Forearms	Curl, Reverse Grip Barbell	12/10/8	1 min./ set	163
Forearms	Curl, Front Wrist	15/12/10	1 min./ set	162
Week three: Tuesday of the Conditioning Phase				
Abdomen	Sit-up, V	3 x 20	1 min./ set	111
Abdomen	Side Bender with Dumbbells	3 x 10 ea	1 min./ set	109
Abdomen	Leg Kick-Alternate	3 x 20	1 min./ set	106
Back	Row Bent-over with Dumbbells or Barbell	12/10/8	1 min./ set	130
Back	Cable Row	10/8/6	1 min./ set	122
Chest	Push-up—Modified	10/8/6	1 min./ set	119
Chest	Bench Press on Incline with Barbell	12/10/8	1 min./ set	114
Shoulders	Press, Seated Dumbbell	12/10/8	1 min./ set	146
Calves	Calf Raise, Seated with Barbell	3 x 15	1 min./ set	134
Week three: Wednesday of the Conditioning Phase				
Triceps	Tricep, Close Grip Bench Press	10/8/6	1 min./ set	154
Shoulders	Press, Seated Dumbbell	12/10/8	1 min./ set	146
Biceps	Curl, Seated Close Grip Concentration Barbell	10/8/6	1 min./ set	159
Forearms	Curl, Reverse Grip Barbell	15/12/10	1 min./ set	163
Forearms	Curl, Reverse Grip Wrist	15/12/10	1 min./ set	164
Calves	Calf Machine	3 x 15	1 min./ set	132

Week three: Thursday of the Conditioning Phase

Legs	Squat	10/8/6	1 min./ set	141
Legs	Squat with Barbell	10/8/6	1 min./ set	142
Legs	Hamstring Curl	12/10/8	1 min./ set	135
Back	Pull, Seated Two Arm Low Lat	10/8/6	1 min./ set	129
Back	Pull, Reverse Grip	12/10/8	1 min./ set	128
Back	Lateral Pull, Close Grip Front	10/8/6	1 min./ set	126

Week three: Friday of the Conditioning Phase

Chest	Bench Press on Incline	10/8/6	1 min./ set	113
Chest	Fly on Flat Bench with Dumbbells	12/10/8	1 min./ set	116
Shoulders	Raise, Seated Side Lateral	12/10/8	1 min./ set	148
Shoulders	Raise-Front with Dumbbells	10/8/6	1 min./ set	147
Shoulders	Row, Upright	10/8/6	1 min./ set	149
Calves	Calf Raise	3 x 15	1 min./ set	133

Week four of the Conditioning Phase

Muscle Group	Exercise	Sets/ Reps	Rest Period	Page

Week four: Monday of the Conditioning Phase

Abdomen	Sit-up on Decline	3 x 15	1 min.	110
Abdomen	Sit-up, V	3 x 15 ea.	1 min.	111
Abdomen	Leg Lift	3 x 12/15	1 min.	107
Triceps	Tricep Extension	12/10/8	1 min./ set	155
Triceps	Cable Push Down on Machine	10/8/6	1 min./ set	151
Biceps	Preacher Curl	12/10/8	1 min./ set	161
Biceps	Curl, Seated Dumbbell	12/10/8	1 min./ set	160
Forearms	Curl, Front Wrist	15/12/10	1 min./ set	162
Forearms	Curl, Reverse Grip Wrist	15/12/10	1 min./ set	164

Week four: Tuesday of the Conditioning Phase

Abdomen	Crunch—Front	3 x 20	1 min./ set	104
Abdomen	Side Bender with Dumbbells	3 x 10 ea.	1 min./ set	109
Abdomen	Leg Kick-Alternate	3 x 20	1 min./ set	106
Legs	Squat	10/8/6	1 min./ set	141
Legs	Leg Extension on Leg Machine	10/8/6	1 min./ set	137
Legs	Hamstring Curl	12/10/8	1 min./ set	135
Back	Row, Bent Over with Dumbbells or Barbell	10/8/6	1 min./ set	130

Back	Cable Row	12/10/8	1 min./ set	122
Back	Pull, Seated Two Arm Low Lat	10/8/6	1 min./ set	129
Calves	Calf Machine	12/10/8	1 min./ set	132

Week four: Wednesday of the Conditioning Phase

Chest	Bench Press on Incline	10/8/6	1 min./ set	113
Chest	Fly on Flat Bench with Dumbbells	12/10/8	1 min./ set	116
Shoulders	Bent Over Raise	10/8/6	1 min./ set	143
Shoulders	Press, Seated Dumbbell	12/10/8	1 min./ set	146
Shoulders	Row, Upright	10/8/6	1 min./ set	149

Week four: Thursday of the Conditioning Phase

Triceps	Tricep Extension, One-handed Dumbbell	10/8/6	1 min./ set	156
Biceps	Preacher Curl	12/10/8	1 min./ set	161
Biceps	Curl, Seated Dumbbell	12/10/8	1 min./ set	160
Forearms	Curl, Reverse Grip Barbell	15/12/10	1 min./ set	163
Calves	Calf Raise Seated with Barbell	15/12/10	1 min./ set	134
Calves	Calf Raise	15/12/10	1 min./ set	133

Week four: Friday of the Conditioning Phase

Legs	Squat with Barbell	10/8/6	1 min./ set	142
Legs	Squat	10/8/6	1 min./ set	141
Legs	Leg Extension on Leg Machine	12/10/8	1 min./ set	137
Back	Pull, Reverse Grip	10/8/6	1 min./ set	128
Back	Pull, Seated Two Arm Low Lat	12/10/8	1 min./ set	129
Shoulders	Press, Seated Dumbbell	10/8/6	1 min./ set	146

Week five of the Conditioning Phase

Muscle Group	Exercise	Sets/ Reps	Rest Period	Page

Week five: Monday of the Conditioning Phase

Abdomen	Sit-up on Decline	3 x 15	1 min.	110
Abdomen	Sit-up, V	3 x 15 ea.	1 min.	111
Abdomen	Leg Lift	3 x 12/15	1 min.	107
Chest	Bench Press on Incline	10/8/6	1 min./ set	113
Chest	Fly on Flat Bench with Dumbbells	12/10/8	1 min./ set	116
Shoulders	Bent-over Raise	10/8/6	1 min./ set	143
Shoulders	Press, Seated Dumbbell	12/10/8	1 min./ set	146
Triceps	Tricep Extension	12/10/8	1 min./ set	155
Triceps	Cable Push Down on Machine	10/8/6	1 min./ set	151

Week five: Tuesday of the Conditioning Phase

Abdomen	Crunch-Open Leg	3 x 20	1 min./ set	105
Abdomen	Side Bender with Dumbbells	3 x 10 ea.	1 min./ set	109
Abdomen	Leg Kick-Alternate	3 x 20	1 min./ set	106
Biceps	Curl, Seated Close Grip Concentration Barbell	10/8/6	1 min./ set	159
Biceps	Preacher Curl	12/10/8	1 min./ set	161
Legs	Squat	12/10/8	1 min./ set	141
Legs	Squat with Barbell	10/8/6	1 min./ set	142
Legs	Hamstring Curl	12/10/8	1 min./ set	135
Calves	Calf Raise, Seated with Barbell	3 x 15	1 min./ set	134

Week five: Wednesday of the Conditioning Phase

Back	Pull, Reverse Grip	12/10/8	1 min./ set	128
Back	Pull, Seated Two Arm Low Lat	10/8/6	1 min./ set	129
Chest	Push-up, Flat Medium Grip	12/10/8	1 min./ set	118
Chest	Bench Press on Incline	10/8/6	1 min./ set	113
Shoulders	Raise, Seated Side Lateral	10/8/6	1 min./ set	148
Shoulders	Raise-Front with Dumbbells	10/8/6	1 min./ set	147
Shoulders	Row, Upright	12/10/8	1 min./ set	149

Week five: Thursday of the Conditioning Phase

Triceps	Tricep Close Grip Bench Press	10/8/6	1 min./ set	154
Triceps	Tricep Extension, One-handed Dumbbell	10/8/6	1 min./ set	156
Biceps	Preacher Curl	12/10/8	1 min./ set	161
Biceps	Curl, Seated Dumbbell	12/10/8	1 min./ set	160
Forearms	Curl, Reverse Grip Barbell	15/12/10	1 min./ set	163
Forearms	Curl, Reverse Grip Wrist	15/12/10	1 min./ set	164

Week five: Friday of the Conditioning Phase

Legs	Squat	10/8/6	1 min./ set	141
Legs	Squat with Barbell	10/8/6	1 min./ set	142
Legs	Leg Extension on Leg Machine	12/10/8	1 min./ set	137
Back	Pull, Seated Two Arm Low Lat	10/8/6	1 min./ set	129
Back	Lateral Pull, Close Grip Front	12/10/8	1 min./ set	126
Back	Pull, Reverse Grip	10/8/6	1 min./ set	128

Things to Remember:

Of course, as with any exercise routine, you need to check in with yourself and get a sense of your personal fitness level. Though the ideal circuit is done without breaks, the beginner, especially one who has been sedentary, might need to pause when necessary. Remember, you will improve and your routine gradually will become easier.

As much as possible, follow the exercise program exactly as it is shown for five weeks, at five sessions per week. It should not take you more than forty-five to sixty minutes per session. Start out by using as much weight as is comfortable, yet challenging, for you for the number of repetitions indicated per exercise set. Your last repetition should feel difficult. Once your sets and repetitions for each exercise become fairly easy to you, increase the amount of weight so that the last repetition is again difficult.

You must breathe during every repetition. Never hold your breath. Exhale on the exertion or first phase and inhale on the return.

If you feel any pain, STOP! Choose a different exercise to work the same muscle group, but one that causes no pain.

Phase Four—The Power Phase

Weeks one through five of the Power Phase

Muscle Group	Exercise	Sets/ Reps	Rest Period	Page
Weeks one through five: Monday of the Power Phase				
Chest	Bench Press on Incline with Barbell	5/5/5	2 min./ set	114
Chest	Fly on Flat Bench with Dumbbells	8/6/5	1 min./ set	116
Back	Row, Bent Over with Dumbbells or Barbell	5/5/5	2 min./ set	130
Back	Pull, Seated Two Arm Low Lat	8/6/5	1 min./ set	129
Legs	Squat	5/5/5	2 min./ set	141
Legs	Leg Extension on Leg Machine	8/6/5	1 min./ set	137
Weeks one through five: Tuesday of the Power Phase				
Shoulders	Press, Seated Dumbbell	5/5/5	2 min./ set	146
Shoulders	Row, Upright	8/6/5	1 min./ set	149
Triceps	Tricep Close Grip Bench Press	5/5/5	2 min./ set	154
Triceps	Tricep Extension	8/6/5	1 min./ set	155
Biceps	Curl, Seated Close Grip Concentration Barbell	5/5/5	2 min./ set	159
Biceps	Curl, Seated Dumbbell	8/6/5	1 min./ set	160
Weeks one through five: Wednesday of the Power Phase				
REST DAY!				

Weeks one through five: Thursday of the Power Phase

Chest	Push-up on Decline	3/2/1	2 min./ set	120
Chest	Bench Press on Incline with Barbell	8/6/5	1 min./ set	114
Back	Row, Bent-over with Dumbbells or Barbell	5/5/5	1 min./ set	130
Back	Pull, Seated Two-arm Low Lat	8/6/5	1 min./ set	129
Legs	Squat	3/2/1	2 min./ set	141
Legs	Hamstring Curl	8/6/5	1 min./ set	135

Weeks one through five: Friday of the Power Phase

Shoulders	Press, Seated Dumbbell	3/2/1	2 min./ set	146
Shoulders	Row, Upright	5/5/5	1 min./ set	149
Triceps	Tricep Close Grip Bench Press	3/2/1	2 min./ set	154
Triceps	Cable Push Down on Machine	8/6/5	1 min./ set	151
Biceps	Preacher Curl	8/6/5	1 min./ set	161
Biceps	Curl, Seated Alternating Dumbbell	8/6/5	1 min./ set	158

Things to Remember:

Be sure to record your progress on the log at the end of this book.

Phase Five–The Maintenance Phase

Week one of the Maintenance Phase

Muscle Group	Exercise	Sets/ Reps	Rest Period	Page
Week one: Monday of the Maintenance Phase				
Chest	Bench Press on Incline	10/8/6	1 min./ set	113
Chest	Fly on Flat Bench with Dumbbells	10/8/6	1 min./ set	116
Shoulders	Row, Upright	8/6/5	1 min./ set	149
Shoulders	Raise, Seated Side Lateral	10/8/6	1 min./ set	148
Shoulders	Press, Seated Dumbbell	8/6/5	1 min./ set	146
Calves	Calf Raise	3 x 15	1 min./ set	133
Week one: Tuesday of the Maintenance Phase				
Legs	Squat	8/6/5	2 min./ set	141
Legs	Squat with Barbell	10/8/6	1 min./ set	142
Legs	Hamstring Curl	10/8/6	1 min./ set	135
Back	Pull, Seated Two Arm Low Lat	8/6/5	1 min./ set	129

Back	Pull, Reverse Grip	10/8/6	1 min./ set	128
Back	Lateral Pull, Close Grip Front	8/6/5	1 min./ set	126

Week one: Wednesday of the Maintenance Phase

Triceps	Tricep, Close Grip Bench Press	8/6/5	2 min./ set	154
Triceps	Tricep Extension, One-handed Dumbbell	10/8/6	1 min./ set	156
Biceps	Curl, Seated Close Grip Concentration Barbell	8/6/5	2 min./ set	159
Forearms	Curl, Reverse Grip Barbell	10/8/6	1 min./ set	163
Forearms	Curl, Reverse Grip Wrist	10/8/6	1 min./ set	164
Calves	Calf Raise	3 x 15	1 min./ set	133

Week one: Thursday of the Maintenance Phase

Chest	Bench Press on Incline	8/6/5	2 min./ set	113
Chest	Fly-back, Lying	10/8/6	1 min./ set	144
Back	Row Bent-over with Dumbbells	10/8/6	1 min./ set	130
Back	Pull, Seated Two Arm Low Lat	8/6/5	2 min./ set	129
Shoulders	Press, Seated Dumbbell	8/6/5	1 min./ set	146
Shoulders	Raise, Seated Side Lateral	10/8/6	1 min./ set	148

Week one: Friday of the Maintenance Phase

Legs	Squat	8/6/5	2 min./ set	141
Legs	Leg Extension on Leg Machine	10/8/6	1 min./ set	137
Legs	Hamstring Curl	8/6/5	2 min./ set	135
Biceps	Preacher Curl	8/6/5	2 min./ set	161
Biceps	Curl, Seated Dumbbell	10/8/6	1 min./ set	160
Calves	Calf Raise Seated with Barbell	3 x 15	1 min./ set	134

Week two of the Maintenance Phase

Muscle Group	Exercise	Sets/ Reps	Rest Period	Page

Week two: Monday of the Maintenance Phase

Chest	Bench Press on Incline	8/6/5	2 min./ set	113
Chest	Push-up—Modified	8/6/5	2 min./ set	119
Shoulders	Press, Seated Dumbbell	8/6/5	2 min./ set	146
Shoulders	Row, Upright	10/8/6	1 min./ set	149
Triceps	Tricep Close Grip Bench Press	10/8/6	1 min./ set	154
Triceps	Cable Curl on Machine	8/6/5	2 min./ set	157

Week two: Tuesday of the Maintenance Phase

Legs	Squat	8/6/5	2 min./ set	141
Legs	Squat with Barbell	8/6/5	2 min./ set	142
Legs	Hamstring Curl	10/8/6	1 min./ set	135
Back	Pull, Seated Two Arm Low Lat	8/6/5	2 min./ set	129
Back	Pull, Reverse Grip	10/8/6	1 min./ set	128
Calves	Calf Raise	12/12/12	1 min./ set	133

Week two: Wednesday of the Maintenance Phase

Biceps	Curl, Seated Close Grip Concentration Barbell	8/6/5	2 min./ set	159
Biceps	Cable Curl on Machine	10/8/6	1 min./ set	157
Triceps	Press Seated Dumbbell	8/6/5	2 min./ set	146
Forearms	Curl, Front Wrist	12/10/8	1 min./ set	162
Forearms	Curl, Reverse Grip Barbell	12/10/8	1 min./ set	163

Week two: Thursday of the Maintenance Phase

Back	Row Bent-over with Dumbbells or Barbell	10/8/6	1 min./ set	130
Back	Rear Flutter Kick	10/8/6	1 min./ set	108
Back	Pull-over Bent Arm with Dumbbell(s)	8/6/5	2 min./ set	117
Chest	Bench Press on Incline	8/6/5	2 min./ set	113
Chest	Push-up, Flat Medium Grip	10/8/6	1 min./ set	118
Shoulders	Press, Seated Dumbbell	10/8/6	1 min./ set	146
Shoulders	Raise-Front with Dumbbells	10/8/6	1 min./ set	147

Week two: Friday of the Maintenance Phase

Legs	Squat	8/6/5	2 min./ set	141
Legs	Squat with Barbell	8/6/5	2 min./ set	142
Legs	Leg Extension on Leg Machine	10/8/6	1 min./ set	137
Biceps	Preacher Curl	10/8/6	1 min./ set	161
Biceps	Curl, Seated Dumbbell	10/8/6	1 min./ set	160
Calves	Calf Raise	3 x 15	1 min./ set	133

Week three of the Maintenance Phase

Muscle Group	Exercise	Sets/ Reps	Rest Period	Page

Week three: Monday of the Maintenance Phase

Chest	Bench Press on Incline	8/6/5	2 min./ set	113
Chest	Fly on Flat Bench with Dumbbells	10/8/6	1 min./ set	116
Shoulders	Press, Seated Dumbbell	8/6/5	2 min./ set	146

Shoulders	Row, Upright	8/6/5	2 min./ set	149
Shoulders	Raise, Seated Side Lateral	10/8/6	1 min./ set	148
Triceps	Press, Seated Dumbbell	8/6/5	2 min./ set	146

Week three: Tuesday of the Maintenance Phase

Legs	Squat	8/6/5	2 min./ set	141
Legs	Leg Extension on Leg Machine	10/8/6	1 min./ set	137
Legs	Hamstring Curl	8/6/5	2 min./ set	135
Back	Row, Bent-over with Dumbbells or Barbell	8/6/5	2 min./ set	130
Back	Pull, Reverse Grip	10/8/6	1 min./ set	128
Calves	Calf Machine	12/10/8	1 min./ set	132

Week three: Wednesday of the Maintenance Phase

Triceps	Tricep Extension	8/6/5	2 min./ set	155
Triceps	Cable Push Down on Machine	10/8/6	1 min./ set	151
Biceps	Curl, Seated Close Grip Concentration Barbell	8/6/5	2 min./ set	159
Biceps	Curl, Seated Alternating Dumbbell	10/8/6	1 min./ set	158
Forearms	Curl, Reverse Grip Barbell	10/8/6	1 min./ set	163
Forearms	Curl, Front Wrist	10/8/6	1 min./ set	162

Week three: Thursday of the Maintenance Phase

Chest	Overhead Press on Machine	8/6/5	2 min./ set	145
Chest	Fly on Flat Bench with Dumbbells	10/8/6	1 min./ set	116
Shoulders	Press, Seated Dumbbell	8/6/5	2 min./ set	146
Shoulders	Raise, Front with Dumbbells	8/6/5	2 min./ set	147
Shoulders	Row, Upright	10/8/6	1 min./ set	149
Calves	Calf Raise	3 x 15	1 min./ set	133

Week three: Friday of the Maintenance Phase

Legs	Squat	8/6/5	2 min./ set	141
Legs	Squat with Barbell	8/6/5	2 min./ set	142
Legs	Hamstring Curl	10/8/6	1 min./ set	135
Back	Pull, Seated Two Arm Low Lat	8/6/5	1 min./ set	129
Back	Pull, Reverse Grip	10/8/6	1 min./ set	128
Back	Row, Bent-over with Dumbbells or Barbell	10/8/6	1 min./ set	130

Week four of the Maintenance Phase

Muscle Group	Exercise	Sets/ Reps	Rest Period	Page
Week four: Monday of the Maintenance Phase				
Chest	Bench Press on Incline	8/6/5	2 min./ set	113
Chest	Fly on Flat Bench with Dumbbells	10/8/6	1 min./ set	116
Triceps	Tricep Extension	10/8/6	1 min./ set	155
Back	Cable Row	8/6/5	2 min./ set	122
Biceps	Curl, Seated Close Grip Concentration Barbell	8/6/5	2 min./ set	159
Forearms	Curl, Reverse Grip Barbell	10/8/6	1 min./ set	163
Week four: Tuesday of the Maintenance Phase				
Legs	Squat	8/6/5	2 min./ set	141
Legs	Leg Extension on Leg Machine	10/8/6	1 min./ set	137
Legs	Hamstring Curl	10/8/6	1 min./ set	135
Back	Pull, Seated Two Arm Low Lat	8/6/5	2 min./ set	129
Back	Row, Upright	8/6/5	2 min./ set	149
Calves	Calf Machine	3 x 15	1 min./ set	132
Week four: Wednesday of the Maintenance Phase				
Chest	Bench Press on Incline with Barbell	8/6/5	2 min./ set	114
Chest	Fly on Flat Bench with Dumbbells	10/8/6	1 min./ set	116
Shoulders	Press, Seated Dumbbell	8/6/5	2 min./ set	146
Shoulders	Raise, Seated Side Lateral	10/8/6	1 min./ set	148
Shoulders	Raise, Front with Dumbbells	10/8/6	1 min./ set	147
Shoulders	Row, Upright	10/8/6	1 min./ set	149
Week four: Thursday of the Maintenance Phase				
Triceps	Tricep Close Grip Bench Press	8/6/5	2 min./ set	154
Triceps	Tricep Extension, One-handed Dumbbell	10/8/6	1 min./ set	156
Biceps	Preacher Curl	8/6/5	2 min./ set	161
Biceps	Curl, Seated Dumbbell	10/8/6	1 min./ set	160
Forearms	Curl, Reverse Grip Wrist	12/10/8	1 min./ set	164
Calves	Calf Raise	3 x 15	1 min./ set	133

Week four: Friday of the Maintenance Phase

Legs	Squat	8/6/5	2 min./ set	141
Legs	Squat with Barbell	8/6/5	2 min./ set	142
Legs	Hamstring Curl	10/8/6	1 min./ set	135
Back	Row, Upright	8/6/5	2 min./ set	149
Back	Row Bent-over with Dumbbells or Barbell	10/8/6	1 min./ set	130
Back	Pull, Reverse Grip	10/8/6	1 min./ set	128

Week five of the Maintenance Phase

Muscle Group	Exercise	Sets/ Reps	Rest Period	Page
Week five: Monday of the Maintenance Phase				
Chest	Bench Press on Incline	8/6/5	2 min./ set	113
Chest	Fly on Flat Bench with Dumbbells	10/8/6	1 min./ set	116
Shoulders	Press, Seated Dumbbell	8/6/5	2 min./ set	146
Shoulders	Row, Upright	10/8/6	1 min./ set	149
Triceps	Tricep Extension	8/6/5	2 min./ set	155
Triceps	Cable Push Down on Machine	10/8/6	1 min./ set	151
Week five: Tuesday of the Maintenance Phase				
Biceps	Curl, Seated Close Grip Concentration Barbell	8/6/5	2 min./ set	159
Biceps	Curl, Seated Dumbbell	10/8/6	1 min./ set	160
Legs	Squat	8/6/5	2 min./ set	141
Legs	Leg Extension on Leg Machine	10/8/6	1 min./ set	137
Legs	Hamstring Curl	8/6/5	2 min./ set	135
Calves	Calf Raise Seated with Barbell	3 x 15	1 min./ set	134
Week five: Wednesday of the Maintenance Phase				
Back	Pull, Reverse Grip	8/6/5	2 min./ set	128
Back	Cable Row	10/8/6	1 min./ set	122
Chest	Bench Press on Incline	8/6/5	2 min./ set	113
Chest	Fly on Flat Bench with Dumbbells	10/8/6	1 min./ set	116
Shoulders	Press, Seated Dumbbell	8/6/5	2 min./ set	146
Shoulders	Raise, Seated Side Lateral	10/8/6	1 min./ set	148
Week five: Thursday of the Maintenance Phase				
Triceps	Tricep, Close Grip Bench Press	8/6/5	2 min./ set	154
Biceps	Preacher Curl	10/8/6	1 min./ set	161
Biceps	Curl, Seated Close Grip Concentration Barbell	8/6/5	2 min./ set	159

Biceps	Curl, Seated Dumbbell	10/8/6	1 min./ set	160
Forearms	Curl, Reverse Grip Barbell	12/10/8	1 min./ set	163
Forearms	Curl, Front Wrist	12/10/8	1 min./ set	162
Week five: Friday of the Maintenance Phase				
Legs	Squat	8/6/5	2 min./ set	141
Leg	Squat with Barbell	8/6/5	2 min./ set	142
Leg	Hamstring Curl	10/8/6	1 min./ set	135
Back	Pull, Seated Two Arm Low Lat	8/6/5	2 min./ set	129
Back	Pull, Reverse Grip	8/6/5	2 min./ set	128
Back	Lateral Pull, Close Grip Front	8/6/5	2 min./ set	126
Calves	Calf Raise Seated with Barbell	3 x 15	1 min./ set	134

Things to Remember:

Follow this weight lifting program for this phase as closely as you can. You need to perform these workout routines for five weeks at five workout sessions each week.

Once you have completed all five phases of the Variable Cyclic Phase System, take a one week rest during which time you do not lift any weights. After this, return to phase three—the conditioning phase, and go through the program again. Complete phase three and go right into phases four and five. Rest, again, for one week after phase five and begin again through the Variable Cyclic Phase System. Each time you go through the program, you should be much stronger, more powerful, and have more endurance.

If you do not increase the intensity of your workout program, you can stay where you are in the program indefinitely. However, change your exercises, sets, repetitions, weights, or any combinations after each phase.

Always use as much weight in your lifting as is comfortable, yet challenging, to you for the repetitions shown in each exercise. The last repetition should be difficult to perform.

CHAPTER 7:
Additional Workout Routines

We already have discussed general principles of working out earlier in this book. Here are different types of routines that could suit you and your time limits and prior commitments. In fact, with some of these routine sessions, you even can work out when you are in a motel room while on vacation.

Additional workout techniques can provide variety, increase resistance, or maximize workout time in your daily workout sessions. They include supersetting and pyramiding.

A superset or compound set occurs when you perform one exercise immediately after the other, with little or no rest until you complete the second set. These supersets usually are performed with opposing muscle groups. For example, the biceps and triceps muscle groups, or the chest and back muscle groups or for the chest from bench press to dumbbell fly, or you might do bench presses (chest) immediately followed by wide-grip pull downs (back), then take a rest period of one or two minutes, followed by the remaining sets. Supersets can reduce workout time and help you to perform more exercises in a given amount of time during your workout sessions. However, you should not begin with them immediately. You need to wait until you are in better physical condition and have more weight lifting experience. You might try this with a group of three exercises performed one after the other, known as trisets.

However, recent studies (O'Shea, 2000) indicate that you may not want to hurry up your lifting. Doing repetitions with lighter weights at about one-third the usual speed forces you to fully contract your muscles but provides an excellent workout, which is safer but harder to do. Another method is to cut each exercise in half. In other words, when lifting, only lift half way and return. This is harder because your muscles have not had a chance to continue the momentum of the movement. Surprisingly, in both cases, doing less will give you more muscle.

With pyramid training, you begin with high repetitions with low weight and then decrease the repetitions as you add weight. The following is an example of a pyramid with bench press:

Sets	Reps	Weight
1	12	150
1	10	175
1	8	200
1	6	225
1	5	250

Note: More reps can be done when using body weight.

Then, you can work your way back down, that is, take off weight and add repetitions. You need to scale your weight, up and down, according to your abilities. You can perform any number of repetitions for the desired number of sets so long as you follow the high repetition/low weight progression to heavier weights with fewer repetitions. If you have hit a plateau where you have not made any gains for a while, then it may be a good idea to try this method. Either add more repetitions with less weight or more weight with fewer repetitions. Gradually, you can build up to a new higher level in both weight and repetitions.

Muscle Group	Exercise	Sets/ Reps	Rest Period	Page
Stomach	Crunch-Front	3 x 20-30	15 sec.	104
Legs	Kick Back Rear	3 x 10-15	30 sec.	136
Calves	Calf Raise	3 x 20-25	30 sec.	133
Chest	Dip	3 x 10-15	30 sec.	115
Back/Biceps	Chin-Up, Front, Close Grip	3 x 10-15	30 sec.	123
Shoulders	Raise Front with Dumbbell	3 x 10-15	30 sec.	147
Triceps	Push-up, Flat Medium Grip	3 x 10-15	30 sec.	118

Occasionally, you should have a little variety in your workout sessions. A systematic change helps both your mental and physical well being. You can substitute this workout routine with other weight lifting routines or even use a combination of both programs. Your imagination is your only limitation.

The intensity of your training is the key to progressive resistance training. For your body to keep responding to the demands made on it, you need to keep increasing the amounts of resistance that you use. There are several ways of doing this:

- Adding more weight. If what you are after is a maximum gain in strength, you should increase the intensity of your training.

- Adding more exercises. This forces your body to perform the same work for longer periods of time. This technique will increase your endurance and cardiovascular conditioning.

Note: The first technique does not have an impact on your conditioning and the second technique is not the best way to increase your strength. Yet, together, they tend to use up an increasing amount of your training time.

However, you might consider another technique—the training circuit. This allows you to do more work in less time. The first step is to remove all the rest periods between sets of exercises. You will perform all of the exercises of this weight training circuit one after the other without stopping for a rest period until you have completed the entire circuit. A continuous training circuit positively increases your intensity. Because it is much more demanding, it will do a lot to greatly improve your strength and endurance (conditioning).

You will have to make some adjustments in your routine when you switch to continuous circuit training. When you go from one exercise to another without stopping, you place much greater demands on your heart and circulatory system than when you stop and take frequent rest periods. Eventually, these extra demands result in a higher level of cardiovascular conditioning. Be aware that when you first begin this type of training, you will tire sooner and, therefore, not be able to lift as much weight. That is normal! After awhile, you will get used to this new routine and will be able to lift even more weight than you were able to before. But you must be patient!

The advantage of this method is that you are able to do more training in less time. Most individuals do not have time for three or four hours to train hard each day, so a program that stresses intensity rather than duration is an answer. Chart 7.1 is a good example of a weight-lifting circuit-workout routine.

Chart 7.1: Weight-lifting Circuit Routine

Muscle Group	Exercises	Reps	Page
Chest	Bench Press on Incline	8-10	113
Chest	Fly on Flat Bench with Dumbbells	8-10	116
Back	Chin-up, Front Close Grip	10-12	123
Back	Row, Upright	8-10	149
Shoulders	Press, Seated Dumbbell	8-10	146
Shoulders	Raise, Seated Side Lateral	8-10	148
Triceps	Tricep Close Grip Bench Press	8-10	154
Biceps	Curl, Seated Close Grip Concentration Barbell	8-10	159
Legs	Squat	8-10	141
Legs	Lunge, Front	8-10	140

There are two additional types of circuit-training programs. One program involves no exercise equipment and the other one uses a Universal Machine or more modern machine.

NO Equipment Program, Muscle Rest, Group Exercise Period

Muscle Group	Exercises	Page
Abdomen	Crunch-Front	104
Chest	Push-up, Flat Medium Grip	118
Lower Abs.	Leg Lift	107
Chest	Push-up Modified	119
Back	Lower Back Stretch	127
Triceps	Dip Off Bench	152
Abdomen	Sit-up, V	111
Chest	Push-up on Decline	120
Abdomen	Leg Kick-Alternate	106
Triceps	Push-up, Flat Medium Grip	118
Oblique	Leg Lift Outside	139
Chest	Push-up-Modified	119

You need to go through this routine nonstop. That is, you may not rest until you have completed the suggested number of circuits. However, like other things, try on your first attempt to complete the first routine but if you cannot, return to this goal on your next regularly scheduled exercise day, and try adding one more exercise each time. Your goal should be to perform three to four complete circuits. However, due to its intensity, you should start this program by completing only one circuit, then two circuits, and then three complete circuits.

For most people beginning this program, use about half the weight you normally would lift.

The Universal Machine Circuit Program

Muscle Group	Exercise	Duration	Rest Period	Page
Leg	Leg Press on Machine	15-30 sec.	JIP	Not Pictured
Abdomen	Sit-up on Decline	15-30 sec.	JJ	110
Chest	Dip	15-30 sec.	JJ	115
Shoulders	Overhead Press on Machine	15-30 sec.	JIP	145
Back	Lower Back Stretch	15-30 sec.	JJ	127
Back	Pull, Reverse Grip	15-30 sec.	JIP	128
Biceps	Cable Curl on Machine	15-30 sec.	JJ	157
Triceps	Cable Push Down on Machine	15-30 sec.	JIP	151
Legs	Hamstring Curl	15-30 sec.	JIP	135

JJ stands for jumping jacks (side-straddle-hop) and JIP represents jogging-in-place.

This circuit program is very demanding and challenging. Instead of working out by using sets and repetitions, you do all exercises within a set time. That is, you will perform each exercise for a certain amount of time instead of depending on the repetitions. Attempt to perform one-quarter of the number of repetitions as the amount of time you are using. Each repetition should take approximately four-to-five seconds. For example, if you are performing bench presses for sixty seconds, then, you should attempt to perform fifteen repetitions and so on for every exercise in the circuit. In between each exercise, you need to continue doing some kind of exercise to keep your heart rate elevated. Hence, the time is nonstop. You should try to perform one complete circuit at the beginning, but your goal should be to attempt to perform three-to-four complete circuits as your physical conditioning improves.

Of course, as with any exercise routine, you need to check in with yourself and get a sense of your personal fitness level. Though the ideal circuit is done without breaks, the beginner, especially one who has been sedentary, might need to pause when necessary. Remember, you will improve and your routine will become easier.

You can consider two approaches when determining when to schedule your workout sessions. The first approach is to exercise your whole body several times weekly. The second approach is to do a split routine, working different body parts on different days.

Beginners should start their training program with the whole body approach. Use your first three-to-six months of training to develop a feel for weight training—to find the groove for different types of exercises. Finding the groove is more a matter of conditioning your mind and body than of building muscle. What you are doing is learning to lift weights correctly and effectively.

During this period, you also are learning how to push yourself hard. As indicated earlier, each muscle is composed of millions of tiny muscle fibers. When you call on a particular muscle, your central nervous system activates only some of those fibers. With experience, you can learn to force your central nervous system to activate more of them. That is why your strength seems to jump drastically during the first six months of lifting. However, if you do not use the days of rest and instead lift weights on those days, you may decrease your overall ability to lift weights. Rest days are vitally important.

In short, the entire beginning stage of lifting is a quest for greater training intensity. You have to learn to put everything you have into each and every repetition you do. To provide your muscles with a sufficient amount of an overload for developing the ability to train intensely, work your entire body each session—especially since, at this stage, you only use one or two exercises per muscle group.

We addressed the subject of how to get started in previous chapters. However, this time there is a different emphasis. If you are a beginner in weight training, you should work the whole body three days weekly (Monday-Wednesday-Friday or Tuesday-Thursday-Saturday). Muscle tissue takes a full forty-eight hours to recover from a heavy workout. If you decide not to skip days in between workout sessions, you run the risk of losing strength and bulk due to insufficient recovery time. Remember, your muscles grow while they rest, not while they are working. Chart 7.2 is an example of a weekly weight lifting routine schedule for beginners.

Chart 7.2 Weekly Weight Lifting Schedule for Beginners

Monday	Tuesday	Wednesday	Thursday	Friday	Saturday	Sunday
Lift	Rest	Lift	Rest	Lift	Rest	Rest

OR

Monday	Tuesday	Wednesday	Thursday	Friday	Saturday	Sunday
Rest	Lift	Rest	Lift	Rest	Lift	Rest

If you consider yourself an intermediate lifter (you have lifted for at least three-to-six months), your training intensity goes up. However, the duration of your workouts must go down. You cannot sprint miles. Likewise, you cannot train at peak intensity for hours at a time. However, as you progress, you will want to add more exercises to your routines for each muscle group. Increased intensity necessitates that you make your workout sessions shorter. Adding more exercises to your routine makes the time of your routine longer.

Split Training Sessions

Split training sessions are an alternative to this problem. You can do either four workout sessions weekly, five workout sessions weekly, or six workout sessions weekly. Spreading your workout sessions over several days decreases the length of time of each session and makes it possible for you to train at a level of high intensity through more exercises per muscle group.

There are various types of split training systems. Here are examples of two.

Training Level	Split	Description	Pattern						
			Day 1	Day 2	Day 3	Day 4	Day 5	Day 6	Day 7
Beginners	none 3 days weekly	whole body whole body	rest	whole body	rest	whole body	rest	rest	whole body
Intermediate	6 day	upper, lower 3 days weekly each	lower body	upper body	lower body	upper body	lower body	upper body	rest
	5 day	upper, lower one 3 days and other 2 days weekly	lower or upper body	upper or lower body	lower or upper body	upper or lower body	lower or upper body	upper or lower body	rest
Advanced	6 day	each muscle group 2 days weekly	lower body	back chest	shoulders arms	lower body	back chest	shoulders arms	rest
	4 day	each muscle group 2 days weekly	lower	upper	rest	lower	upper	rest	rest

Remember, you cannot make muscular gains unless you make excessive demands on your muscles. This is an inflexible rule! Nature will not allow your muscles to grow unless your body makes a strong and intense effort through your weight training program. Not understanding this principle of weight lifting is the primary reason many weight lifters are unable to make satisfactory progress. Many weight lifters think that they can make their muscles grow bigger by doing more work—more sets and more exercises. However, the opposite is true. Doing too many sets or too many exercises can stop all of your weight lifting progress. This results in overtrained muscles. Overtrained muscles are not going to get bigger. The most intense effort will provide you with the most in muscular gains.

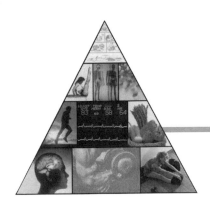

CHAPTER 8:
Cardiovascular Conditioning

Weight training alone is not enough. It must be accompanied by aerobic activity—also known as endurance. Together, weight training and cardiovascular conditioning is known as total fitness. The objective is to receive the benefits of sustained motion—being physically active without tiring too quickly. Alas, golf and bowling do not qualify as aerobic activities because there is not a sustained rhythmical activity involved.

Total fitness requires you to work out to strengthen your heart, which can be done through a variety of methods. The heart is just like other muscles, the more you use it, the stronger it becomes. But, you cannot launch into exercise immediately if you have been sedentary. However, you can begin by walking. Walk to the store rather than drive. Walk during your break rather than sit down and drink coffee. You will be surprised how this provides you with more energy even when you feel tired.

If you include planned, sustained exercise, not only will you develop more energy, it will improve your cardiovascular health. This means that you will increase the ability of your heart and blood vessels to supply oxygen to your body. This additionally increases your body's volume of blood and increases your lung capacity to transport oxygen into the blood and remove the waste products or carbon dioxide from the blood. In return, you get increased stamina. It decreases your body fat. And, it reduces your stress and tension. Couple this with good nutrition and you have a winning combination. It is best to keep track of the amount of aerobic activity that you get.

People tend to procrastinate and then think they have done what they should—often even when they have not done it. Yet, if we have written down exactly what we have done, we can see our progress in keeping with the program. Also, as we noted in the introductory chapters, this aerobic activity is critical for correctional officers who are prone to heart attacks and strokes.

Eventually, you will be able to substitute an increased number of repetitions of the exercises or the circuit training used in this program for some of the aerobic activity.

However, in the beginning fitness stages, it is important to have other aerobic activities that you engage in with regularity.

Another reason for doing aerobic activity is the natural high that you feel when you exercise. You probably have heard about runners who run to get the benefit of the release of endorphins. You can have this experience as well. Most people continue to exercise aerobically to get this benefit. Unlike drugs, the amount of exercise you need to reach this high does not increase with time. However, when you cannot exercise, you may begin to feel a bit despondent. This can be alleviated when you resume exercising.

How do you know if you have gotten your heart rate up enough to gain the benefit of exercising? You can use a simple technique: if you are unable to carry on a normal conversation while exercising, you need to take it easier—your heart rate is too high.

Consider what type of exercises you will be doing to meet your cardiovascular needs. The requirements for cardiovascular exercise are that the exercises should be performed at a relatively low intensity to enable you to continue to exercise rhythmically approximately thirty-to-sixty minutes at a time.

These cardiovascular exercises should be performed at least five to seven times weekly in addition to your other training for a desirable training effect to occur according to the Surgeon General's Report (U.S. Department of Health and Human Services, 1996). Before starting any strenuous cardiovascular exercise program, check with your physician—especially if you are more than fifty-five years of age, are overweight, under a large amount of stress, or if you have not exercised for a while.

The following items are yellow lights that indicate you should proceed with caution. If you fit into any of the following categories, it is especially crucial that you check with your doctor. The following items may not stop your exercise regime, but your doctor may suggest some modifications to help you avoid problems.

- Are you a couch potato—do you lead a life with little or no exercise? This is an important consideration especially if you are more than thirty-five years of age and critical if you are overweight by twenty or more pounds. Being older, no matter how you define it, is no excuse not to exercise. In fact, doctors recommend older people pump iron to build up their muscle mass. Exercising causes hormones to circulate; that helps in this process.

  See the suggested height-weight charts on pages 11–12.

- Are you a smoker or do you have any history of lung disorders or asthma?

- Are you regularly taking any prescription medication, including but not limited to insulin? Regular exercise lowers the risk factors for type 2 diabetes. Are you regularly taking any other over-the-counter medications? These, too, may have an impact on your exercising.

- What about your heart? No, not your love life, but the basic pumping mechanism of your body? Are you ever short of breath with little or no exertion? Your doctor may recommend getting an electrocardiogram or a stress test that shows a picture of your beating heart before you begin. Sometimes heart problems may be hidden and individuals may not be aware of them until they stress their heart with exercise. Better safe than sorry. In some cases, severe dizziness or fainting may be related to circulation or heart problems. Is there a family history of heart problems? What about your blood pressure? Is it too high? Regular physical activity lowers the risk factors for cardiovascular disease and helps control blood pressure.

- How out of sight is your cholesterol? If you do not know, it is time to get it tested. Exercise can have a beneficial impact on your cholesterol but a high level of the bad cholesterol (HDL) may indicate some other medical problems that require medical intervention.

- Do you have any special aches and pains when you move in certain ways? What old injuries or strains do you have? Again, often there are ways to accommodate these problems but it is important to do this before you begin rather than be sidelined with major problems later.

- How dense are your bones? If you are over forty-five, you may want to get a bone scan that can provide some useful information. This is especially important if any of your relatives have osteoporosis. Even if they do not, such information is important because it can make the difference between being bent over and shriveled up when you get older and being able to stand erect.

You need to monitor your pulse throughout all of your exercise sessions—especially during cardiovascular exercises. The cardiovascular training effect occurs when you work your heart muscle at 60 to 85 percent of its maximum heart rate. The maximum heart rate is the fastest that your heart can beat and still efficiently pump blood to your body. You can use the following method to determine what your training effect is and the way to monitor your heart rate during exercise:

1. Subtract your age from 220.
2. Multiply that number by 60 to 85 percent.
3. Adjust this number to suit your goals.

For example, If you are forty: $220 - 40 = 180$

$180 \times 70 = 126$ Beats Per Minute

$180 \times 85 = 153$ Beats Per Minute

Your training rate in this example ranges from 126 to 153 beats per minute during exercise for the cardiovascular conditioning that you want.

To monitor or check your pulse rate, place your index and middle fingers across your wrist. Either count the beats for fifteen seconds and multiply that number by four or count the beats for six seconds and multiply that number by ten. Either way you should be within the range of your cardiovascular training effect. You should discover an improvement in your cardiovascular condition as your training increases.

However, the exercise indicated here must be sustained over a longer period of time than a brief break from work. You should do an aerobic activity for at least thirty minutes three-to-seven times per week. This can include running, walking briskly or on a treadmill, bicycling, swimming, or anything else that gets the heart pumping and the lungs working for a sustained period of time. This can include dancing, skating, or a range of other activities. The objective is to receive the benefits of sustained motion—being physically active without tiring too quickly.

For example:

Monday	Tuesday	Wednesday	Thursday	Friday	Saturday	Sunday
Week 1						
Weights	Run	Weights	Walk	Weights	Bicycle	Rest
Week 2						
Walk	Weights	Run	Weights	Bicycle	Weights	Hike

Alternate the Week 1 schedule with the Week 2 schedule.

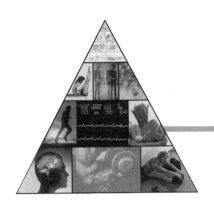

CHAPTER 9:
Stretching

Benefits of Regular Stretching

Stretching elongates your muscle fibers. When you feel sore after exercising, it is because you have stretched your muscles more than they previously have been stretched. Some people prefer the stretches in yoga practice to those given here, and that is fine. Yoga is a method of disciplined stretching. Stretching also should be done after exercising and may be done between sets.

After a warm up, you might do stretching exercises for five minutes, do your regular exercises, then do stretching exercises at the end for three to five minutes. The final stretching exercises are particularly important.

Stretching is a fundamental part of any sensible exercise routine. It can aid in increasing flexibility as well as preventing injury. If you have ever seen a runner pressing up against a building, and wondered what that was all about, it is called *stretching*. Without it, the runner would be in danger of pulling or straining a muscle or tendon.

Stretching should be seen as the noncaloric icing on the cake. It does a variety of good things for you but does not interfere with your becoming fit. Indeed, it helps in that goal. Stretching reduces the tension on muscles. It increases your flexibility, which in turn aids in coordination while increasing the range of your motion. Because you have greater flexibility, stretching prevents injuries and increases circulation. It also makes strenuous activities easier. Stretching after lifting aids you in relaxing the stress on the muscles and hence reduces soreness. Often, it is a natural reflex that helps you feel the exercise has been completed.

How often should you perform stretches? There is no hard and fast rule about this. Like much in exercise, it depends when you are stretching and why you are stretching at that particular time. If you are stretching before you get into your physical fitness regimen, you might consider three to five repetitions for about fifteen seconds each. Your body will begin to respond and you can stop the stretch when you feel a pull on the muscles that you are seeking to stretch. If you hold each stretch a bit more, for an additional ten-to-twenty seconds until you feel a slight tension again, you get an additional stretch. This increases your flexibility and prepares your muscles for the exercises that follow.

Stretching should be done slowly while you stay in control. There should be no jerking or bouncing movement. As in all exercise, if you feel any pain, relax and loosen up or stop. Be sure to breathe throughout the stretch. Never hold your breath. Another idea to help you gain flexibility is a massage, which may be welcome both before and especially after exercising.

Stretching can be meditative. By stretching slowly, you can encourage a calm peacefulness. Let your mind and body relax. Perhaps change the music you use. As with all exercise, do not wear clothing, shoes, or a belt that restricts your range of motion.

Remember, stretches should be done before you begin exercising and after you are done. You should do a stretch for each muscle group you are going to exercise. For some of the muscle groups, we have provided a choice. As you gain experience, you will begin to feel which muscles need to be stretched. It is an excellent idea also to stretch between sets of an exercise. The stretches in this section are arranged according to order of the exercises from abdomen, thighs, chest, back, shoulders, to triceps, and biceps. Do not think you are saving time by eliminating the stretches. This is akin to only eating steak and neglecting the other parts of the meal.

Pre-Exercise Stretching

Warm up for a few minutes before you begin stretching. The warm up may include doing a low level of the exercise you will be doing, walking, slow jogging, or riding an exercise bike, marching in place, or doing knee lifts. Then, add upper body warm-up work such as shoulder shrugs where you elevate your shoulder blades then lower them. Backstrokes are another upper body warm up where you pretend you are swimming and move your arm like a windmill going backwards.

Basics for Stretching

- Stretch the specific muscles you need for the sport or activity, plus do a general stretch of the major muscle groups.
- Move rhythmically between stretching, which is why music is good to have in the background when you work out.
- Focus on the muscles you want to stretch. Again, visualization can help.
- Breathe during a stretch.

Stretching After Exercising

After exercising, you have warmed up your body and just stopping your exercise may allow the muscles to tighten up and lead to muscles soreness. Stretching helps to prevent this. This is especially important for people who are new to exercise.

Types of Stretching Techniques

There are several types of stretches. All stretches lengthen the muscle fibers. We will provide examples of several types of stretches. However, there are many other types that you can do.

STRETCHES FOR CONDITIONING AND TRAINING

Total Body Stretch

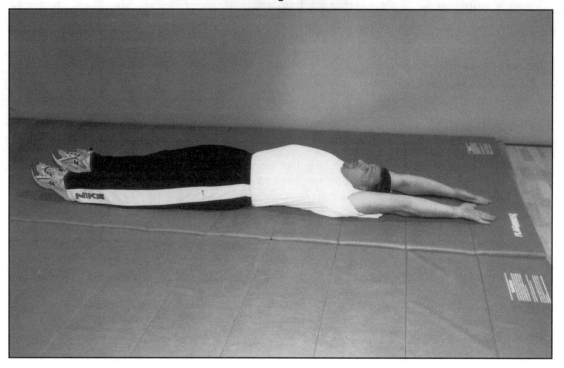

1. Lie on your back on a mat on the floor.
2. Fully extend your arms above your head and point your toes.
3. Inhale and hold.
4. Exhale and relax.

Note: This stretch is good both at the beginning and at the end of your workout.

The Cobra (Bhujangasana)

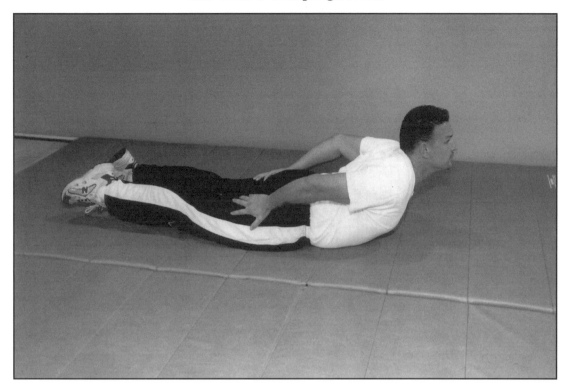

Welcome to the world of yoga with a wonderful stretch for the arm, chest, shoulders and back.

1. Lie on your mat on the floor, face down, forehead lightly touching the floor.
2. Inhale and gently lift your upper torso off the floor, raising your chest and head.
3. Hold the pose for a few breaths, exhaling on the way down.
4. The more advanced you are, the more flexible you become and the greater your range of motion. Start small, and increase your movement gradually.

The Bow (Dhanurasana)

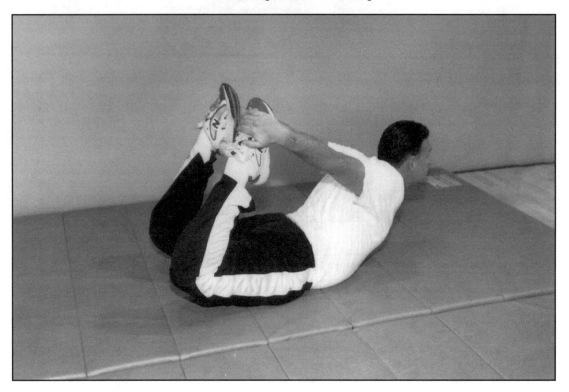

More yoga based exercise! This one is good for stretching the back, but proceed with caution if you have lower back problems.

1. Lie on the floor on your mat, flat on your belly.

2. Bend your legs at the knee and bring your feet toward your rear end, grabbing onto the mid section of your shoes.

3. Gently lift off the floor, hold for a few seconds, then return to the starting position.

Ankle Pull Stretch

This benefits your thigh muscles.

1. Lie on your stomach on your mat with one leg straight and the other bent at the knee at a ninety degree angle.

2. Put a towel around the bent leg and hold it with your hands behind your back.

3. Raise your neck and shoulders off the ground.

4. Try to straighten your bent leg but feel the pull from the towel until the thigh is tight.

5. Hold it for a few seconds.

6. Relax.

7. Switch legs and repeat the stretch.

Calf Stretch-A

This is a good exercise for runners and those doing leg exercises.

1. Stand tall, and place your right leg behind you. Your left knee will be bent. Tuck in your abdominals.

2. Place your hands on your left knee and stretch. (The right leg is being stretched.)

3. Keep your hips parallel and maintain a proper spinal alignment.

4. Hold the stretch for a count of ten, and repeat on the other side.

Calf Stretch-B

This strengthens and stretches the calves and the Achilles tendons.

1. Position yourself as though you were pushing the wall.
2. Stand facing the wall about two feet away from it.
3. Brace your hands with your palms out about shoulder height on the wall with elbows relaxed.
4. Step the right leg behind the left leg and bend the knee of the left leg slightly. Keep the heel intact with the floor.
5. Switch legs and repeat the stretch.

Note: This stretch is good for working out pain in the calves, so it may be particularly useful at the end of the workout.

Cross Knee Twist Stretch

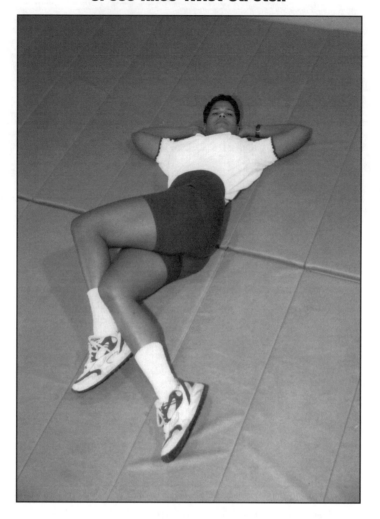

This benefits your hips and lower back.

1. Lie flat on your back on a mat on the floor with your arms on the floor straight out to the side.

2. From the bent-knee position, lightly touch the back of your head with your fingers behind your head.

3. Keep your abdomen tight and your neck straight.

4. Place your left knee over your right knee.

5. Use the weight of your left leg to pull your right leg toward the floor until you feel a stretch along the side of your hip and lower back.

6. Stretch from this position and then relax.

7. Keep your upper back, shoulders, and elbows as flat on the floor as possible.

8. You do NOT have to touch the floor with your right knee, only stretch within your limits.

9. Hold the position for ten-to-twenty seconds.

10. Repeat this stretch on the other side.

Leaning Side Stretch

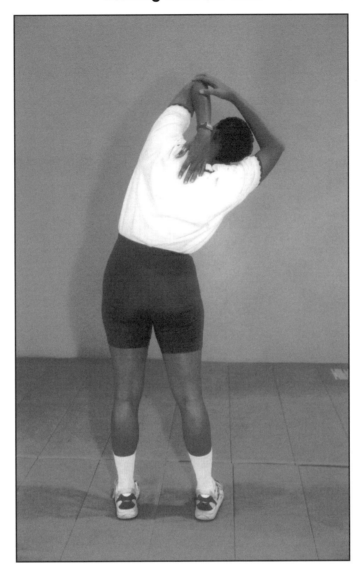

1. While standing, place your arms overhead and hold the elbow of one arm with the other hand.

2. Keeping your knees slightly bent, gently pull your elbow behind your head as you bend from your waist to the right side.

3. Hold this stretch for ten-to-twenty seconds.

4. Repeat this stretch on the left side.

Note: Keeping your knees slightly bent will provide better balance.

Lunge Stretch

This stretch helps relieve tension in your lower back.

1. From a standing position, slowly move toward the floor placing the left leg forward until the knee of your forward leg is directly over your ankle.

2. Rest your back knee on the floor.

3. Without changing the positions of your feet and legs, lower your hips downward to create an easy stretch.

4. You should be able to feel this stretch in your front hip and possibly in your hamstrings and groin areas.

5. Hold this position for fifteen-to-thirty seconds, then switch to your right leg.

Lying Knee High Stretch

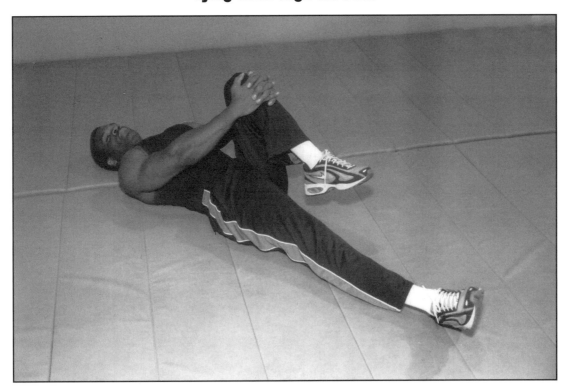

This benefits your abdomen and thighs.

1. Lie flat on the floor on your mat on your back.

2. Straighten both legs and relax.

3. Tighten your abdomen.

4. Keep your neck straight and your back pressed to the ground. Inhale.

5. Pull your left knee toward your chest. Grasp your knee underneath with your hands.

6. Keep the back of your head on the floor.

7. Hold this position for ten-to-twenty seconds.

8. Repeat the exercise by pulling your right knee toward your chest.

Note: You may start this stretch with your knees bent and your feet flat on the floor. You also may decide to lift both knees simultaneously with your hands holding the back of your thighs.

Overhead Stretch

This is a good stretch anytime or anywhere for you upper back.

1. In either a standing or seated position, interlace your fingers above your head.
2. Place your palms upward and push your arms slightly back and up.
3. You should feel the stretch in your arms, shoulders, and upper back.
4. Hold the stretch for fifteen-to-thirty seconds.
5. Do not hold your breath.

Rear Upper Body Stretch

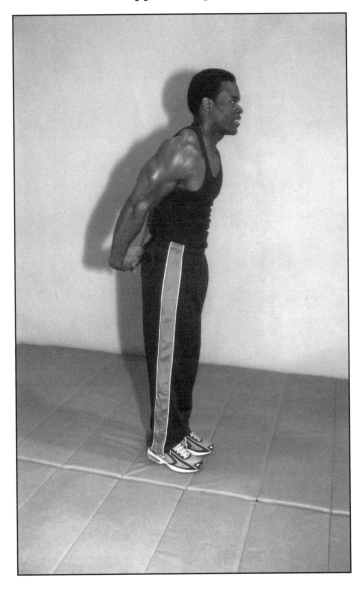

This is an excellent stretch for your shoulders and arms.

1. You may perform this stretch from either a standing or a leaning position.
2. Interlace your fingers behind your back.
3. Keep your abdominals tucked in.
4. Slowly turn your elbows inward while you straighten your arms.
5. Hold this position for ten-to-twenty seconds.

Seated Side Twister

This will stretch your lower back and the side of your hip.

1. Sit on the floor on your mat with your left leg straight out.
2. Bend your right knee and place your right foot outside of your left knee.
3. Bend your left elbow and place it outside of your upper right thigh, just above your right knee.
4. During your stretch, use your elbow to keep controlled pressure to the inside.
5. Place your right hand on the floor behind you.
6. Slowly turn your head to look over your right shoulder.
7. At the same time, rotate your upper body toward your right hand and arm.
8. Hold this position for ten-to-twenty seconds and repeat the stretch on the other side.

Seated Single-leg Stretch

This stretches your hamstrings.

1. Place your rear end on the floor and straighten your right leg
2. Place the bottom of your right foot next to the inside of your left leg.
3. Lean slightly forward from your hips and stretch the hamstrings on your left leg. Inhale as you stretch.
4. Find the point in your stretch that is comfortable, exhale and relax.
5. If you cannot touch your toes comfortably, use a towel around the bottom of your foot.
6. Hold this stretched position for fifteen-to-thirty seconds.
7. Do NOT lock your knee (flex it) and keep the joint relaxed.
8. Your right quadriceps should be relaxed.
9. Keep your left foot upright with your ankle and toes relaxed.
10. Repeat this exercise with your other leg.

Standing Quadriceps Stretch

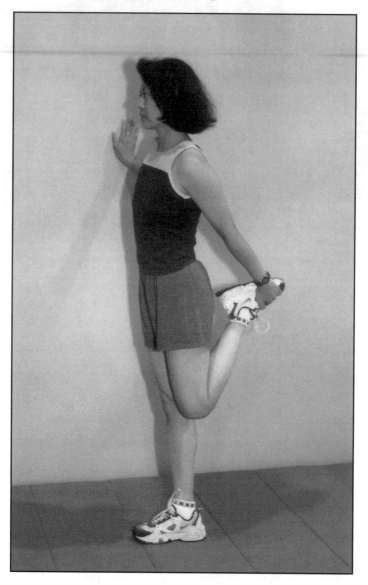

This benefits your quadriceps.

1. From a standing position, place your right hand on an immovable object (such as a wall) to hold your balance.

2. Bend your left knee and move your left foot up toward your rear end.

3. Place your left hand around the top of your left foot and gently pull your left heel towards your rear end.

4. Your knee will bend at a natural angle, which will create a good stretch in your knee and quadriceps.

5. Hold this stretch for fifteen-to-thirty seconds and switch feet and hands.

6. Do not hold your breath.

Straddle Sit

This is an excellent stretch for your ankles and Achilles tendons, groin, lower back, and hips.

1. Place your feet about shoulder width apart and pointed outward at approximately a fifteen to twenty degree angle.

2. Bend your knees and squat down—push your rear end out as though you were sitting on the toilet—but keep your back straight and your stomach tight.

3. If you cannot sustain this position, hold onto an object that provides you with support.

4. Hold this stretch for fifteen-to-thirty seconds.

5. Do not hold your breath.

Note: If you have knee problems, be careful. If you feel pain, STOP!

Straddle Stretch

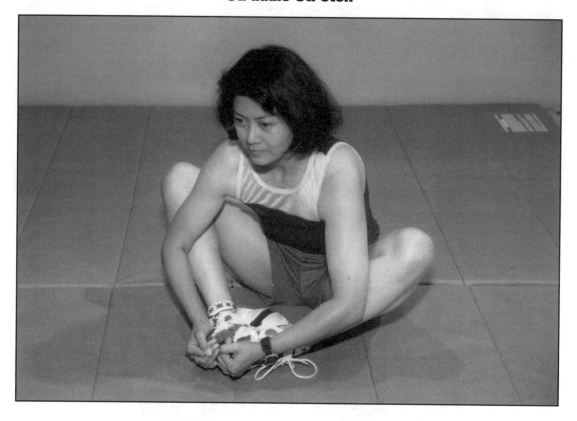

This stretches your inner thighs.

1. Sit on the floor on your mat with the bottoms of your feet together with your heels a comfortable distance from your groin.

2. Place your hands on your feet and slowly lean forward from the hip joint until you feel an easy stretch in your groin area.

3. Bend forward from your hips, not from your shoulders, by keeping your back straight.

4. If you possibly can, keep your elbows outside of your lower legs for stability.

5. Hold this stretch for ten-to-twenty seconds.

Upper Back Stretch

This stretch will take some of the tension off your tired upper back

1. Place both your hands about shoulder width apart on a wall, fence, or ledge.
2. Allow your body to drop down as you maintain a slight flex in your knees.
3. Insure that your hips are directly over your feet.
4. To change the focus of your stretch, bend your knees slightly more and/or place your hands in a different position (higher or lower).
5. Find a stretching position you feel comfortable with and hold it for fifteen-to-thirty seconds.
6. Do not hold your breath while performing this stretch.

Note: Remember, bend your knees when you finish this stretch.

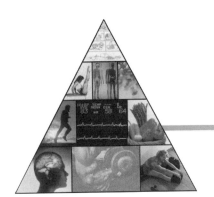

CHAPTER 10:
Exercises for Your Whole Body

EXERCISES FOR YOUR ABDOMEN

Often this area is called simply "the abs." Technically, it is the upper and lower transverse abdominus. The abdominals support the upper body from the lower body. Excess fat in your abdominal area puts a strain on your lower back, causing back pain. Abdominal muscles help move your legs and shift your hips. Visualize your abs as an accordion, which can expand and shorten. It is one muscle, though some exercises strengthen the upper part and others strengthen the lower part. The sides, called the obliques, are commonly known as your "love handles." They run diagonally both internally and externally. They aid in bending and supporting your spine and are necessary for good posture.

Perform the abdominal exercises until fatigued. Stay in control. Do the exercises slowly. Jerking, bouncing, or lunging could lead to injuries.

When you get more advanced, the order of abdominal exercises should be from the lower abs, progressing to your external and internal obliques, and finishing up with your upper abs (Meja, 2000). *See* the muscle pictures on pages 49–50.

Crunch—Front

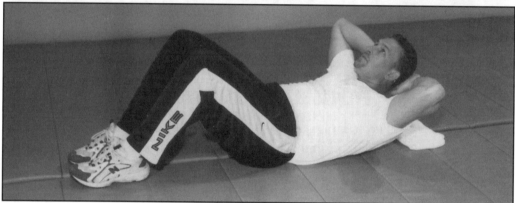

This is one of the most effective exercise for strengthening your upper and lower abdomen and preventing lower back pain.

1. Lie on your back on your exercise mat, knees bent, with feet flat on the floor, approximately hip-width apart, about six inches from your rear.

2. Place your hands behind your head, with fingers supporting the back of your head and thumbs at ear level. Do not join hands or lock fingers. The function of the hands behind the head is simply to provide support for the neck, not to pull on the neck. The origin of the movement of the crunch occurs at the waist.

3. With elbows out to the sides, tilt your chin towards your chest but not directly on the chest. Keep your neck aligned with your spine.

4. With a fluid movement, lift your shoulder blades slightly off the floor. Be sure your lower back stays on the mat.

5. Feel the contraction in your abs.

6. Hold for a few seconds, then release and return your shoulders to the starting position.

7. Exhale as you rise up, and inhale on the return down.

Note: This may be performed with your legs at a ninety degree angle, or you may rest your legs on a chair or bench. In some versions of this exercise, after the lift, your hands return toward your feet. This exercise may be performed on a crunch machine. As your abs get stronger, you can place a light weight across your chest as you do the exercise.

Crunch—Open Leg

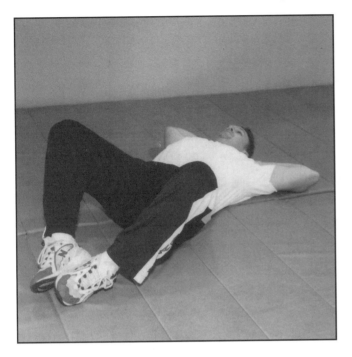 

This is good for your upper and lower abs. It is a variant on the prior exercise.

1. Lie on your back on your exercise mat, knees bent out to the side and the soles of your feet together. Keep your knees as close to the floor as possible.

2. Place your hands behind your head, with fingers supporting the back of your head and thumbs at ear level. Do not join hands or lock fingers.

3. With your elbows out to your sides, tilt your chin towards your chest but not directly on the chest. With a fluid movement, lift your shoulder blades slightly off the floor. Be sure your lower back stays on the mat. Curl your pelvis slightly up and in.

4. Feel the contraction in your abs.

5. Hold this position for a few seconds, then release and return your shoulders to the starting position.

6. Exhale as you rise up, and inhale on the return down.

Leg Kick—Alternate

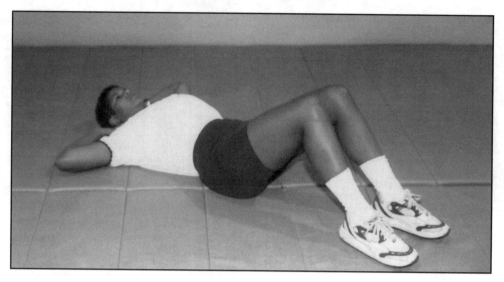

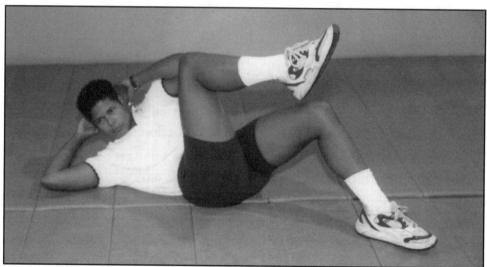

This tightens, tones, and defines the lower abdominal area and helps to strengthen your lower back.

1. Lie on your exercise mat. Bend your knees with your feet flat on the floor.
2. Place your hands behind your head and gently lift your shoulders off the floor.
3. Lift one leg into a ninety-degree position, while exhaling and lift the opposite shoulder toward that leg.
4. Hold the position for a few seconds.
5. Inhale as you return to the starting position.
6. Switch sides and repeat the exercise.
7. Alternate your left and right sides.

Leg Lift

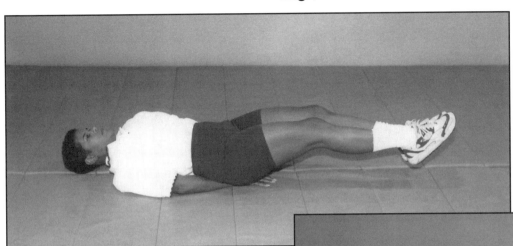

This exercise tightens, tones, and defines the lower abdominal muscles and strengthens the lower back.

1. Lie on the floor on your exercise mat with your hands under your rear end, your palms down, and your legs extended slightly off the floor.

2. Bend your knees and pull them into your chest. Keep your body flat on the floor.

3. Suck in your lower abdominal muscles, keeping the small of your back against the mat.

4. Return to the starting position.

5. Concentrate on your lower abdominal area. Inhale while you move your feet up, and exhale while you move them down.

Notes:

- *There are several variations to this exercise. To make this exercise more challenging, place a lightweight dumbbell between your feet.*

- *This exercise can be done on an incline bench but when doing it, hold onto something that will keep you from moving down on the board, such as a rope or handle at the top of the board.*

- *Another variation is done sitting on the end of your flat bench and you grasp the sides of your bench near your rear end.*

- *A further variation is to lift your left knee while your right leg is slightly lifted. Hold, then straighten your leg to the starting position and repeat with the other leg.*

Rear Flutter Kick

This benefits your obliques and lower back.

1. Sit on the floor on your hands and knees.
2. Extend the left leg behind your body, keeping your heel aligned with your knee and your knee aligned with you hip.
3. Pull your leg in (towards your chest) maintaining proper alignment.
4. After exercising on the left leg, switch to the right leg and repeat this exercise.
5. Remember to exhale on the effort and inhale on the return.

Side Bender with Dumbbells

This is good for the oblique muscles, or "love handles" on the side of your abdomen.

1. Stand erect with your feet together.

2. Place a dumbbell in each hand with arms along the side of your body.

3. Bend to the right as far as possible from the waist and then bend to the left as far as possible.

4. Keep your back straight and your head facing the front.

5. Bend at the waist only, not at your hips or knees. Keep your head steady.

6. Inhale as you bend and exhale as you return.

7. Repeat the exercise and perform the same number of reps on each side.

Note: You can do this exercise seated. For variety, do this exercise with a barbell.

Sit-up on Decline

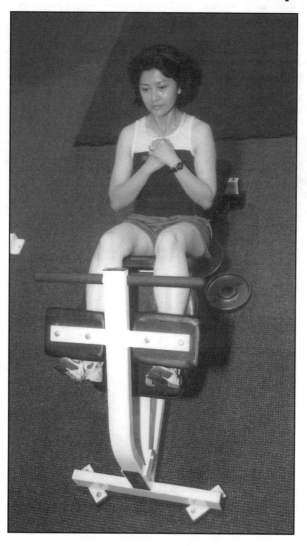 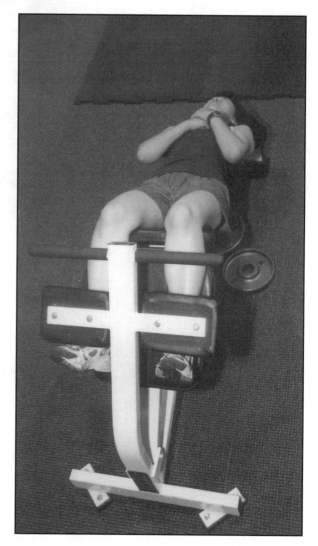

This benefits your abdominals.

1. Lie down on a decline bench with your knees slightly bent, and your lower leg anchored (have someone hold them, if necessary) and your hands across your chest.

2. Bend at the waist and sit up.

3. Then, return to the starting position before repeating the exercise.

4. Exhale on the rise up, and inhale on the return.

Sit-up, V

This benefits your upper and lower abdominals.

1. Lie on the floor on your exercise mat on your back with your legs raised in a V form.

2. Place your arms above your head.

3. Bend at your waist, and at the same time, raise your arms and legs so they meet in a "V" position.

4. Tuck in your abs.

5. Lower your arms and legs to the floor at the same time.

6. Exhale while you move up, and inhale on the return.

7. Do not lock your arms or legs in the exercise.

Twister with Broom Handle—Seated

This benefits your oblique muscles.

1. Place a broom handle on your shoulders.

2. Sit down on the end of your bench and place your feet firmly on the floor.

3. Twist your upper body to the right, then to the left by twisting from your waist only.

4. Keep your head facing the front—do not move it from side to side.

5. Keep your back straight and your head up.

6. Exhale while you move to the right, and inhale on the return.

7. This exercise also may be performed while you are standing.

EXERCISES FOR YOUR CHEST

Bench Press on Incline

This benefits your chest.

1. Lie back on the incline bench with your head higher than your feet. Plant your feet firmly on the ground.
2. Hold a dumbbell in each hand, with your palms facing up.
3. The outer edge of the dumbbell should almost touch your upper chest.
4. Flex your chest muscles as you extend your arms upward until your elbows are nearly locked.
5. Flex your pectoral muscles and gently bring the weight down toward your chest by bending your elbows.
6. Repeat the movement by raising the dumbbells above your head.
7. Exhale as you press the weights up, and inhale as you return them down.

Note: This exercise also may be performed with a barbell, or on the straight exercise bench. This exercise can be performed using a barbell with either a wide grip (hands are greater than shoulder width apart—about six-to-eight inches outside the width of your shoulders, which benefits your inner chest and triceps muscles) or a close grip (hands are eight-to-ten inches apart, which benefits your outer chest muscles).

Bench Press on Incline with Barbell

This benefits your upper chest.

1. Lie on your exercise bench in the incline position.
2. Grasp the barbell with your hands shoulder width apart and your feet firmly placed on the floor.
3. Take the bar off the bench uprights and lower the bar down to your chest plate (just below the collarbone). Keep the motion smooth. Be careful not to snap your elbows
4. Raise the barbell up extending your arms. Keep your elbows relaxed.
5. Lower the weight with complete control and make a slight pause at your chest before pushing the weight back up to arms length.
6. Keep your head on the bench and do not arch your back.
7. Do not raise your hips off the bench.
8. Inhale while you lower the barbell, and exhale while you raise the barbell.

Note: This exercise can be performed with either a close or a wide grip. In a wide grip, the hands are greater than shoulder width apart. This exercise also may be performed in a decline bench position, which benefits your lower chest.

Dip

This benefits your shoulders, chest, and triceps.

1. Hold yourself erect on the dip bars (you also can use the backs of two solid chairs).

2. While keeping your elbows into your sides, lower your body by bending your elbows and shoulders.

3. Lower yourself down as far as you can so your feet are off the floor. It is okay to bend your legs and cross your legs at the ankle. Do not go lower than having your chest parallel with the bars.

4. Pause at the bottom and push yourself back up to arms length.

5. Do not allow your body to swing back and forth.

6. Inhale while you lower yourself down, and exhale while you push yourself up.

Note: Dips are push-ups on parallel bars.

Fly on Flat Bench with Dumbbells

This develops, shapes, strengthens and defines the entire chest, especially the upper pectoral area.

1. Lie on your back on your exercise bench.
2. Hold dumbbells in your hand at arms length, above your shoulders, palms facing each other.
3. Open your arms out to the sides of your chest, with your elbows relaxed.
4. Repeat the motion by returning to the starting position.
5. Inhale as you open and exhale as you push your arms back together.

Note: This also may be done on an incline bench.

Pull-over Bent Arm with Dumbbell(s)

This benefits your upper chest, rib cage, and triceps.

1. Lie on your back on your exercise bench or mat with your feet firmly on the floor and your head at the end.
2. Raise your arms with a dumbbell in each hand <u>or</u> using both hands grip one dumbbell. Keep your elbows slightly bent.
3. Raise your arms over your head.
4. Lower the dumbbells as close to the floor as possible or as low as is comfortable.
5. Pull the dumbbells back to your chest using the same path.
6. Inhale as you lower the dumbbells and exhale as you return.
9. Do not raise your hips off the bench.

Push-up, Flat Medium Grip

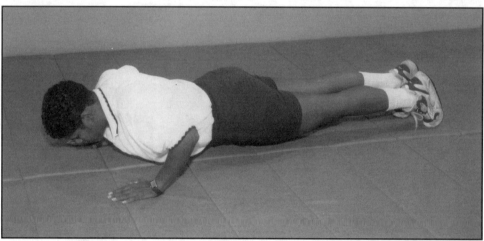

This benefits your chest or pectorals and triceps.

1. Lie on your stomach on the floor.
2. Place your hands on the floor about twenty-four inches apart with your palms down.
3. Put your legs straight out behind you about ten-to-twelve inches apart.
4. Keep your back straight and your head up.
5. Keep your body rigid and lower yourself until your chest is about one-to-two inches off the floor.
6. Pause slightly at the bottom and press up to the starting position.
7. Repeat this for the number of reps indicated.
8. Inhale while you lower yourself down, and exhale while you push yourself up.
9. Tuck your elbows in throughout the exercise.

Note: This exercise can be performed with varying grips (wide-to-narrow), and with your feet up on your bench or on a chair (Push-up on Decline), or with your upper body higher than your feet (Push-up on Incline).

Push-up—Modified

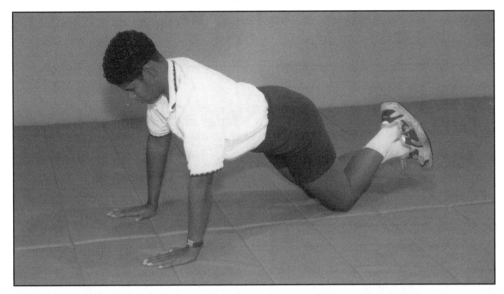

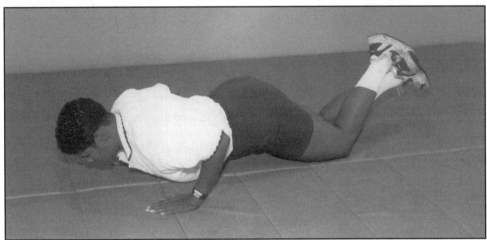

This benefits your upper body, especially your pectorals and triceps.

1. Place your palms face down on the floor about twelve inches apart.
2. Bend your knees and cross your feet at the ankle with your knees close together.
3. Pull in your abdominals and tuck in your chin. Keep your back straight.
4. Bend your elbows and begin to lower yourself toward the floor.

Note: It is not necessary to touch your chest to the floor.

5. Contract your abdominals, rear end, and lower back.
6. Raise yourself up and repeat the movement.
7. Exhale when rising up, and inhale while lowering yourself.

Note: Maintain proper spinal alignment and do not allow your lower back to dip.

Push-up on Decline

This benefits your pectorals and triceps.

1. Carefully place your feet over an exercise bench behind you.
2. Place your hands more than twelve inches apart with your palms down.
3. Keep your head forward and your back straight.
4. Gently relax your elbows and lower yourself down until you almost can touch the floor; then, raise yourself up.
5. Exhale as you push up, and inhale as you go down.

Exercises for Your Back

The back is the reverse side of the abdominals. When you do an abdominal exercise, you also should do a back exercise to work its opposing muscle group.

The back is the key to your strength and mobility. However, back pain can wreak havoc with your mobility. Generally, the most serious back pain stems from the six muscle groups that support the upper, middle, and lower back. To prevent back pain, it is vital to do stretching and flexibility exercises to take away some of the stress and tension. Crunches for the abdominals and exercises for the obliques also help.

Note: Back exercises are pull exercises and you exhale during the pull (exertion) while you inhale on the return.

Cable Row

This benefits your back.

1. With a bar attachment on a low pulley, sit with your feet straight in front of you, pressed against the block.
2. With abdominals pulled taut, and knees slightly bent, grasp the handle firmly and pull the bar to your lower chest, elbows slightly behind you.
3. Keep your back straight while holding this position for a few seconds.
4. Slowly reverse the motion, and return to the starting position.
5. Exhale on the pull, and inhale on the return.

Note: This exercise can be performed one hand at a time, if you attach a horseshoe grip to the pulley.

Chin-up, Front Close Grip

This benefits your lower lats.

1. Use a chinning bar that is high enough off the floor so that there is no interference.

2. Grasp the chinning bar with your hands six-to-eight inches apart. Your palms face you. Cross your legs behind you and lift them up.

3. Pull your body up until your chin touches the bar or an area where the bar would be.

4. Return to the starting position.

5. Do not swing back and forth.

6. Try to hang perfectly still while you are performing this exercise.

7. Exhale while you pull-up, and inhale while you lower yourself down.

Note: You also may do this exercise with a medium grip, with your hands about eighteen-to-twenty inches apart.

Dead Lift, Stiff-legged with Barbell

This benefits your obliques and lower back.

1. Stand erect with your feet greater than shoulder width apart.
2. Keep your shoulders back and your chest out; push your rear end out.
3. Grasp a barbell with both hands.
4. Keep your back straight, head up, hips locked, and your knees slightly flexed.
5. Using only the muscles in your back, slowly lower the weight to the floor.
6. Exhale while you move up and inhale on the return.

Note: Using a broomstick or unweighted barbell rather than dumbbells allows you to develop the proper form, especially if your hamstring muscles are tight.

Dead Lift, Stiff-legged with Dumbbell—Cross Over

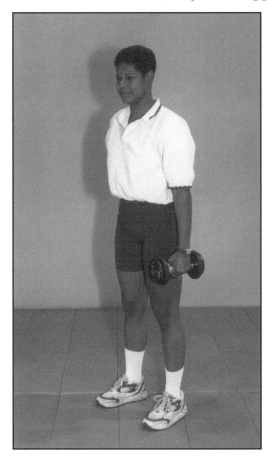 

This benefits your oblique and lower back muscles.

1. Stand erect with your feet greater than shoulder width apart.
2. Grasp a dumbbell with your left hand, palm facing inward.
3. Place your right hand on your right hip. Do not lock your knees.
4. Bend forward until the dumbbell nearly touches your right foot (or as far as you can bend comfortably).
5. Return to the starting position.
6. Change the dumbbell to your left hand and repeat the exercise.
7. Inhale while you move down, and exhale while you move up.

Note: This exercise also may be performed with a barbell.

Lateral Pull, Close Grip Front

This benefits your lower lateral muscles, called lower "lats."

1. Grasp the bar on the cable with your palms facing away from you and about eight-to-ten inches apart.

2. Kneel down or sit down low enough to support the weight.

3. Extend your arms overhead.

4. Pull the bar straight down until it is below your chin.

5. Push your arms up and begin again.

6. Inhale while you pull the bar down, and exhale while you move it up to the starting position.

Lower Back Stretch (also known as the Superman Stretch)

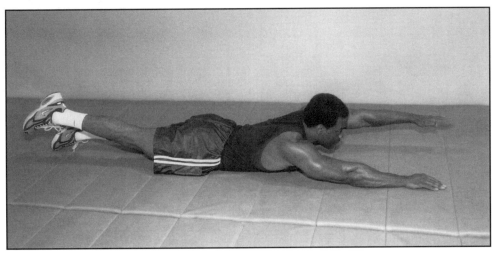

1. Lie down on your mat on the floor face down.

2. Inhale, tuck in abdominals, and begin to gently lift your hands and legs off of the floor at the same time. (This is where the Superman stuff comes in).

3. Try and raise yourself another inch or so, and then return to the starting position.

4. Once you get the hang of this, try alternating arms and legs: left arm, right leg. Return to the starting position and then lift your right arm and left leg.

Pull, Reverse Grip

This benefits your back.

1. Get comfortable on the lat pulldown machine.
2. Make adjustments for your legs.
3. Stand up and grab the bar and then sit down. For shorter people; it is okay to stand on the seat to reach the bar before you sit down.
4. Hold the bar in a reverse, overhand grip (your palms facing you), and slowly bring the bar down to slightly below the collar bone.

Note: Do not hyperextend the movement nor try to create a large a range of motion.

5. Slowly bring the bar back to the starting position.
6. Exhale on the pull down, and inhale on the return.

Pull, Seated Two Arm Low Lat

This benefits your lower lats and upper back.

1. Sit on the floor in front of the low-cable attachment.
2. Brace your feet against some stationary object for support.
3. Grasp the low pulley handles in your hands.
4. Bend forward slightly throughout the exercise.
5. Do not move back and forth at the waist.
6. Pull the handles directly to the sides of your chest.
7. Return to the starting position.
8. Inhale at the beginning of the pull, and exhale at the end.

Note: This exercise also can be performed using one arm at a time.

Row, Bent-over with Dumbbells or Barbell

This develops, strengthens, shapes, and defines your upper and lower lats and helps develop your biceps.

1. Place the dumbbell on the floor next to your bench.
2. Stand with left knee on the exercise bench and right leg on the floor.
3. Place the opposite hand (as the leg on the bench) on the bench, bending at the waist. Keep standing with your right leg slightly bent.
4. Bend over at your waist and grasp a dumbbell in your right hand with your palm in.
5. Keeping your back straight, pull the dumbbell up and in towards your body, so it rests touching your bent-over chest. Your elbow should be pointing toward the ceiling.
6. While using the same path and movement, return to the starting position.
7. Exhale as you pull your arm up and inhale as you go down with the dumbbell.
8. Once you have performed the necessary number of repetitions with your right arm, change the dumbbell to your left hand and repeat the exercise with the opposite leg.

Note: You may use the lat pulldown machine in place of this exercise. You may do a similar exercise with a barbell.

EXERCISES FOR YOUR THIGHS, LEGS—INCLUDING CALVES, AND REAR END

Thighs and legs are crucial for those in corrections where walking around is part of the job. Legs obviously are critical for your work and used in almost every sport. In the front of the thighs are the quadriceps that guide your lower body. On the inside and outside of your thighs are the abductor and adductor muscles that run up to the hip and help you close your legs and move out to the side. On the back of your thighs are the hamstring muscles. They help you in kicking and stabilize the knees. The lower part of the leg contains the calf muscles that provide stability and balance and help you move your feet and stabilize your ankles.

Your ankles are where your leg and foot bones are connected. Ankles can be damaged by wearing the wrong shoe for an activity, which makes you unbalanced. Cross trainer shoes are recommended for weight lifting.

The rear end contains the gluteal muscles. Strong gluteal muscles are important for your mobility, especially around the hips. They let you rotate and extend your legs. They also help to alleviate lower back pain. Many leg exercises automatically strengthen the gluteal muscles. These include lunges, squats, and leg presses.

Calf Machine

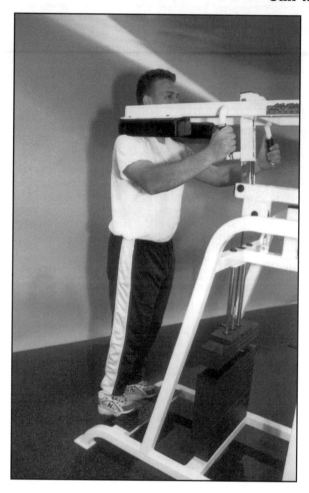 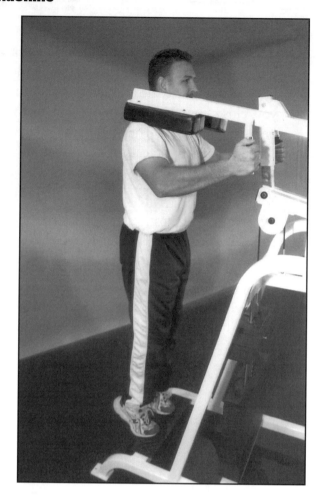

This benefits your calf muscles.

1. Position your shoulders under the pads of the calf machine.
2. Stand erect with the balls of your feet on the foot pads of the calf machine.
3. Keep your back straight and your head up.
4. Keep your knees relaxed.
5. Do not allow your hips to move back and forth.
6. Raise up on your heels as high as possible.
7. Hold the position for a moment and return to the starting position and repeat.
8. Exhale while you raise up, and inhale while you lower yourself.

Calf Raise

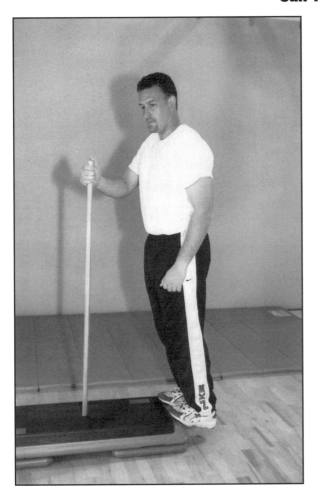 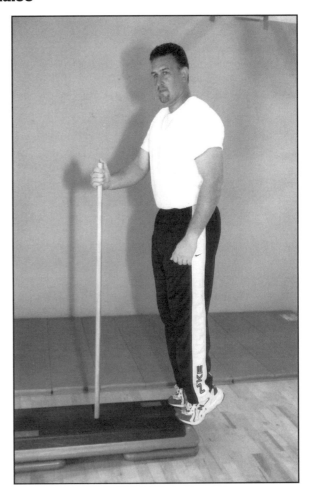

This benefits your calves.

1. Stand on a step or on an aerobics platform.
2. Place the balls of your feet at the edge of the step, while your heels hang off.
3. Tuck in your abdominals.
4. If necessary, hold onto a wall or stick for support.
5. Slowly raise your heels a few inches off the ground, balancing your weight on your tiptoes.
6. Gently lower your heels below the starting position. Then, repeat the movement.
7. Exhale as you raise, inhale on the lowering.

Note: As you gain proficiency, add dumbbells to your lowered arms as you do this exercise. To exercise one leg at a time, tuck one leg behind you by bending your knee, and exercise on the standing leg. When finished, alternate your legs. See the seated version of this, Calf Raise Seated with Barbell on page 134.

Calf Raise Seated with Barbell

This benefits your calf muscles.

1. Place a two-inch by four-inch piece of wood, fat book, or riser on the floor about twelve inches away from the end of the bench.
2. Sit at the end of your exercise bench with your heels off the platform.
3. Place the barbell on your upper legs about three inches above your knee.
4. Put the balls of both feet on the two-inch by four-inch piece of wood or book.
5. Point your toes straight ahead. Flex your calf muscles as your raise your heels.
6. Raise your heels up slowly as high as you possibly can and hold the position for a moment, and relax.
7. Return to the starting position.
8. Exhale while you raise your heels up, and inhale while you lower them.

Note: This exercise can be performed one leg at a time using a single dumbbell. It also may be performed on a seated calf machine. You may wish to strengthen the inner thigh area by doing this exercise with your toes pointed outward.

Hamstring Curl

This exercise tightens, tones, shapes, and defines the back thigh muscles (the biceps) and the hamstrings.

1. Lie face down on your exercise mat with your arms extended out by your ears and forearms supporting your head.
2. Place a dumbbell between your feet, squeezing your ankles together.
3. Extend your legs straight out behind you.
4. Bend your knees, flexing your hamstrings as you pull your heels toward your rear end.
5. Return to the starting position.
6. Exhale as you pull (bending your knees) and inhale on the return.

Note: This exercise may be performed one leg at a time. A variation on this is the leg curl machine with either a single or a double leg.

Kick Back Rear

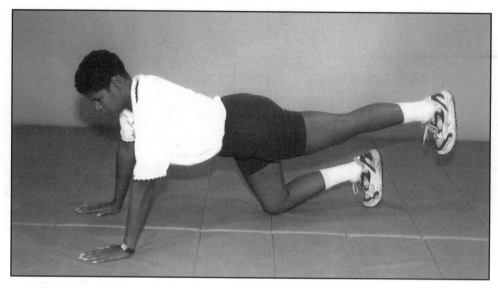

This tightens and tones the complete hip and rear end.

1. Kneel on your left knee on a flat bench or on the floor.

2. Hold the outer sides of your bench or balance yourself on the floor. Keep your elbows relaxed.

3. Raise your left leg straight back no higher than parallel to your body. Pause. Flex your toes forward.

4. Do NOT bend your raised knee. Flex your left rear end muscle. Keep your body still.

5. Return your leg to its starting position.

6. Repeat the exercise with your right leg.

7. Exhale as you extend your leg and inhale as you return.

Note: This exercise also may be performed standing up.

Leg Extension on Leg Machine

This benefits your lower thighs.

1. Sit on the end of the leg extension machine with your feet under the lower foot pads.
2. Place your knees against the back of your seat.
3. Hold the seat behind your rear end.
4. Point your toes slightly downward.
5. Raise the weight up until your legs are parallel to the floor.
6. Contract your quadriceps. Do not lock your knees when your legs are fully extended.
6. Return to the starting position and repeat.
7. Exhale while you raise the weight up, and inhale while you lower it down.

Note: To work the muscles more, do this one leg at a time.

Leg Lift–Inside

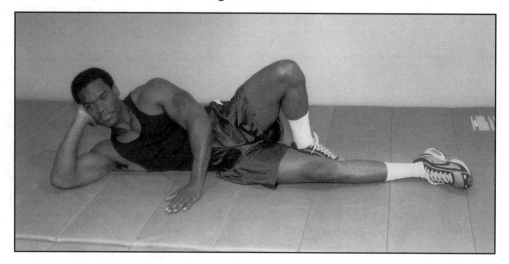

This helps to tighten and tone your inner thigh muscles, the quadriceps.

1. Lie on your exercise mat on your right side.
2. Extend your right leg and bend your left leg and place your left foot flat on the floor in back of your right leg.
3. Support your head with your right hand, balancing on your left hand.
4. Raise your right leg as far as you can. Flex your thigh muscle.
5. Keep your knee straight but not locked.
6. Do not bend at your waist.
7. Return your leg to the starting position. Do the number of repetitions indicated.
8. Turn over and lie on your left side and repeat this with your left leg for the number of repetitions indicated.
9. Exhale while you raise your leg, and inhale as you lower it.

Leg Lift-Outside

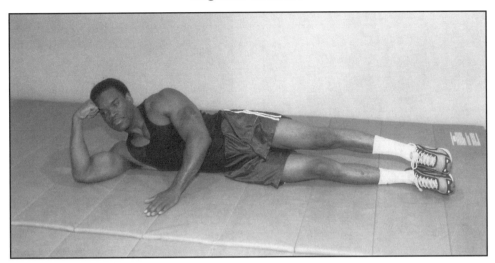

This benefits your outer hip–your obliques.

1. Lie on your right side with both legs outstretched.
2. Support your head with your right arm.
3. Lift your left leg up and back slowly.
4. Keep your knees straight with your toes slightly pointed down.
5. Raise your leg about eighteen inches.
6. Hold this position for a moment.
7. Slowly, lower your leg.
8. Do the number of reps on one side before turning over and doing the same on the other side.

Note: To make this lift more difficult, you can place a dumbbell on the thigh of the working leg.

Note: This exercise also can be performed while standing. You may wish to hold onto some support while doing it in this way. Alternatively, this exercise may be performed on an outer thigh machine.

Lunge, Front

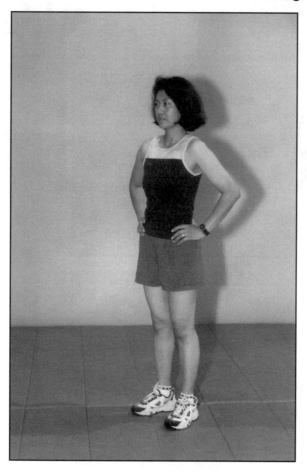 

This exercise tightens, tones, and defines the front thigh muscles (the quadriceps) and hamstrings and helps to tighten the rear end.

1. Stand straight with your feet about twelve-to-fourteen inches apart. Put your hands on your hips.

2. Keep your back straight and your head up.

3. Fluidly move your right leg as far forward as possible until your upper thigh is almost parallel to the floor. Bend at the knee as you lunge. Keep your knee aligned with your heels. Feel the stretch in your front thigh as you finish.

4. Keep your left leg back and bent at the knee. Your left heel will come up slightly.

5. Step back to the starting position and repeat with your left leg. Flex your quadriceps.

6. Exhale while you step forward, and inhale while you step back.

Note: This exercise may be performed with a light barbell bar on your shoulder or with dumbbells hanging straight down from your sides with your arms fully extended. You may substitute a leg press for this exercise.

This exercise can be added to all phases after phase one, the preparatory phase, to provide a thigh exercise.

Squat

 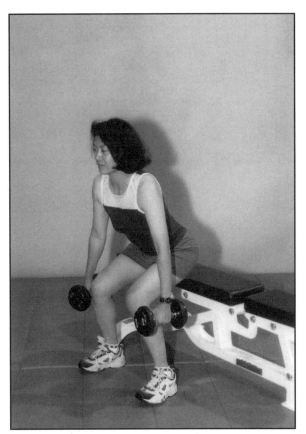

This benefits your upper thighs.

1. Put the exercise bench or a chair behind you so that your heels are even with the end of the bench or chair.

2. Grasp the dumbbells to your sides at arms length with your palms in.

3. Keep your head up and your back straight, lean slightly forward from the hip joint.

4. Place your feet firmly at a distance greater than shoulder width apart.

5. Squat down until your rear end almost touches the bench.

6. Almost sit down on the bench. Keep tension on your thighs throughout the exercise.

7. Return to the starting position and repeat.

8. Inhale while you lower yourself down, and exhale while you raise yourself up.

Note: This exercise can be performed with dumbbells your heels elevated on a two-by four-inch piece of wood or while free standing without a bench or chair.

This exercise also may be performed with a barbell behind and across your upper shoulder muscles with your palms facing forward, or it may be done by holding the bar palms-up, hands shoulder width apart. Your elbows should point forward as the barbell rests across your upper chest (See Squat with Barbell page 138).

Add this exercise to any of the routines after phase one to provide a thigh exercise.

Squat with Barbell

This develops, shapes, strengthens, and defines your front thighs (quadriceps), and helps tighten and tone the rear end and legs.

1. Place the barbell on the upper part of your back (be sure to keep the bar away from your neck).

2. Use a comfortable hand grip (place a towel or other soft pad between your back and the barbell).

3. Keep your head up and your back as straight as possible.

4. Place your feet flat on the floor at a distance slightly greater than shoulder width apart.

5. Squat down until your upper thighs are parallel to the floor but no lower; otherwise, you can hurt your knees.

6. Keep your head up and your back very straight. Lean slightly forward from the hip joint.

7. Press up with your thighs to the starting position.

8. Inhale while you lower yourself down, and exhale while you raise yourself up.

Note: If squats are difficult or cause you pain, do another exercise that does not hurt you.

EXERCISES FOR YOUR SHOULDERS

Bent Over Raise

This develops, shapes, strengthens, and defines the rear and side shoulder (deltoid) muscles.

1. Sit at the end of the exercise bench (flat) with a dumbbell in each hand.

2. Bend forward from the hip joint so that your back is approximately parallel to the floor.

3. Tuck in your abdominals and tuck your chin into your chest.

4. Slowly raise your arms to your sides, bend your elbows, and raise your arms until they are level with your shoulders.

5. Hold this position for a few seconds, while squeezing your shoulder blades together.

6. After completing your range of motion, gently return to the starting position.

7. Exhale on the raise, and inhale on the return.

Note: This may be performed standing. Alternatively, you may perform this exercise on a floor pulley machine.

Fly-back, Lying

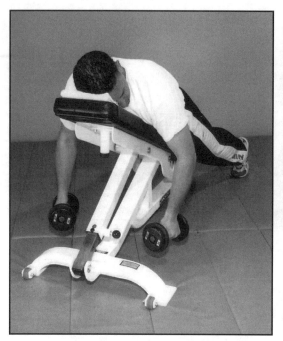 

This benefits your mid back.

1. Lie on your stomach on your incline exercise bench with your shoulders, arms, and legs hanging off.

2. Hold a dumbbell in each hand with your elbows slightly bent and palms facing each other.

3. Lift the dumbbells up to shoulder height.

4. Pull your shoulder blades together and keep your elbows up. Keep your neck aligned with your spine.

5. Return to the starting position.

Overhead Press on Machine

This benefits your front and outer deltoids.

1. Sit erect on the floor cross-legged under the bench press on the bench press machine.

2. Grasp the bar with your hands shoulder width apart and the bar slightly above your shoulders.

3. Press the bar upright as far as your arms can reach.

4. Lower the bar to the starting position.

5. Exhale as you raise the bar, and inhale as you lower it.

Press, Seated Dumbbell

This benefits your front and outer deltoids

1. Sit at the end of your exercise bench with the dumbbells held at shoulder height, and your feet firmly on the floor.

2. With your palms facing inward, press the dumbbells overhead at arms length.

3. Hold for a second or two, then return to the starting position and repeat.

4. Keep your elbows in throughout the exercise.

5. Exhale while you press the dumbbells up, and inhale while you lower them down.

Note: For variation, slowly raise the dumbbells overhead until they almost touch. This exercise also can be performed with palms out and/or with a barbell held on the upper chest or behind the head.

Raise, Front with Dumbbells

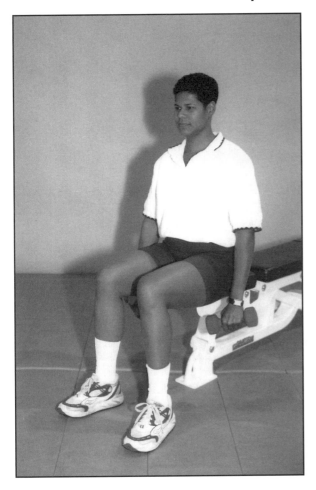 

This benefits your shoulders.

1. Sit at the edge of the exercise bench, with your feet firmly planted on the floor.
2. Grab each dumbbell with an overhand grip, and bring the weights to approximately shoulder level in front of you.
3. Hold for a second or two.
4. To complete the exercise, return the weights to the starting position.
5. Exhale on the effort, and inhale on the return

Note: You may do this exercise standing with your feet ten inches apart. This exercise also may be performed by alternating the dumbbells. In other words, raise one arm up while the other arm is down and then reversing the movement. Or, you may use a barbell instead of dumbbells, using both arms at the same time.

Raise, Seated Side Lateral

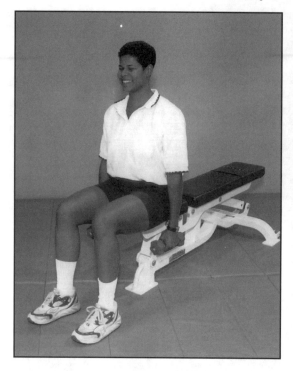 

This develops, shapes, strengthens, and defines your front and medial deltoids.

1. Sit at the end of your exercise bench and place your feet firmly on the floor.

2. Hold a dumbbell in each hand with your palms in and your arms straight down at your sides.

3. Flexing your shoulder muscles, raise the dumbbells up to a position parallel with your shoulders.

4. Flex your shoulders. Pause at the top and lower the dumbbells to the starting position following the same path down.

5. Keep your arms straight and your elbows slightly flexed. Be careful to stay in charge and not swing the dumbbells.

6. Exhale while you raise the dumbbells up, and inhale while you lower them down.

Note: This exercise also may be performed from a standing position, or on a shoulder side lateral machine. You may perform this exercise one arm at a time on a floor pulley device.

Row, Upright

This develops, shapes, strengthens, and defines the complete trapezius muscle and also strengthens and defines the front shoulder muscle.

1. Stand tall, feet shoulder width apart, a dumbbell in each hand resting comfortably at your thighs.
2. With elbows out, tuck in your abdominals.
3. Raise dumbbells to almost chin level, elbows toward your ears.
4. Flex your trapezius muscles. Hold the position for a few seconds.
5. Concentrate on the integrity of the movement, keeping your upper body steady and weights flush to your body.
6. Flex your shoulder muscle on each upward movement and feel the stretch on each return down.
7. Lower the dumbbells to the starting position and repeat the exercise.

Note: You may use a shoulder press machine in place of this exercise and you may use one or two arms at a time. Alternatively, you may use a barbell for this exercise, or you may use a floor pulley.

Shoulder Shrug with Dumbbells

 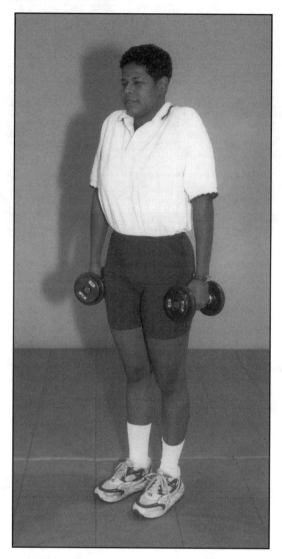

This benefits your upper back or trapezius muscles, called "traps."

1. Keep your feet apart.
2. Grasp your dumbbells with your palms in.
3. Stand erect, with the dumbbells hanging down at arms length at your sides.
4. Droop your shoulders downward as low as possible.
5. Raise your shoulders as high as possible.
6. Exhale as you lift your shoulders and inhale on the return.

Note: This exercise may be performed with a barbell.

EXERCISES FOR YOUR TRICEPS

Cable Push Down on Machine

This benefits your triceps.

1. Stand facing the machine, feet shoulder width apart, arms at sides, knees slightly bent.
2. Grab the straight bar handle attached to the cable, forearms parallel to the floor at approximately ninety degrees.
3. Tuck in your abdominals and take a deep breath.
4. Slowly push the bar down, elbows close to your sides.
5. Hold this position for a few seconds, then slowly release and return to the starting position.
6. Exhale on the downward motion, and inhale on the upward motion.

Note: A one-armed cable push down also can be performed by replacing the straight bar handle with a horseshoe. This time, place the nonworking arm on your hip for balance and support. For variation, you can use a Lat Machine (dual arm).

Note: If you are exercising at home without a machine, you can mimic this exercise by using a Dynaband or other elastic band gym equipment, which is available at most fitness stores. With free weights, you also can try a dumbbell triceps curl, either in a standing or a sitting position.

Dip Off Bench

This benefits your triceps.

1. Sit at the edge of the exercise bench (you should begin at the center of the long end of the bench)

2. Place your arms behind you and grasp the edge of the bench, then slide off the bench, keeping your legs straight down, on a nice long angle.

3. Tuck in your abdominals and gently lower yourself so that your upper arms are nearly parallel to the floor.

4. When you have completed your range of motion, reverse and return to the starting position.

5. Exhale on the effort, and inhale on the return.

Kickback

This develops, shapes, strengthens, and defines the complete triceps.

1. Hold a dumbbell upright with your left hand with your palm facing inward.
2. Sit at the end of your exercise bench with your feet firmly placed on the floor.
3. Lean over as far as possible. Grasp your knee with your right hand.
4. Draw your upper arm to your side and leave your lower arm vertical with the floor.
5. Flex your triceps as you press the dumbbell back until your entire arm is parallel to the floor.
6. Hold the dumbbell in this position for a moment.
7. Lower the dumbbell slowly to the starting position.
8. Keep your upper arm as close to your side as possible and level with your back.
9. Exhale while you raise the dumbbell up, and inhale while you lower it down.
10. Repeat the exercise with your right arm. Alternate arms until you have completed the required number of reps.

Note: This exercise may be performed while you are bent over and standing. It also may be performed using two dumbbells. Alternatively, you may do this exercise on any high pulley device or on the lat machine.

This benefits your triceps.

1. Lie flat on your back on the exercise bench with your feet flat on the floor.

2. Grasp the barbell with hands side by side less than shoulder width apart.

3. Lower the bar until it slightly touches about one inch below the midlevel of your chest.

4. Press the barbell back to its starting position and repeat.

5. Keep your elbows as close to your sides as possible.

6. Inhale while you lower the barbell down, and exhale while you raise it up.

Tricep Extension

This develops, shapes, and defines your triceps.

1. Lie on your back on your exercise bench.
2. Grasp the barbell with your hands about six-to-eight inches apart with your palms up.
3. Press the bar to arms length directly above your shoulders.
4. Bend your elbows, lowering the bar towards your head.
5. Return to the starting position. Flex your triceps muscles.
6. Inhale while you lower the barbell down, and exhale while you push the barbell up.

Note: This exercise may be performed with a medium grip or while lying flat on the floor. It also can be performed while using two dumbbells with your palms facing inward or while using an E-Z Curl bar.

Tricep Extension, One-handed Dumbbell

This exercise develops, shapes, strengthens, and defines your complete triceps muscles.

1. Sit at the edge of your exercise bench, your feet flat on the floor.
2. With a dumbbell in your right hand, extend your right arm overhead.
3. Keep your elbow slightly in front of your ear.
4. Inhale as you bend your elbow bringing the weight down behind your head.
5. Exhale as you extend your arm to return back to the starting position.
6. Repeat the exercise with the other arm.

Note: This exercise may be performed with two dumbbells with your palms facing inward. It also may be performed from a chair, or while you are lying down on an incline bench with either a barbell or with two dumbbells.

EXERCISES FOR YOUR BICEPS

Cable Curl on Machine

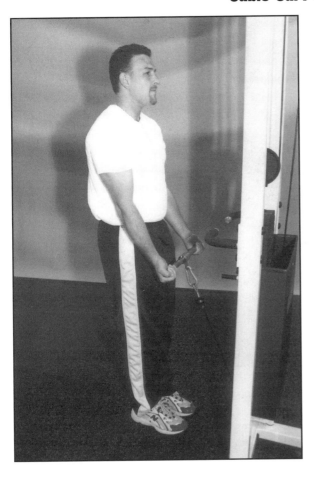 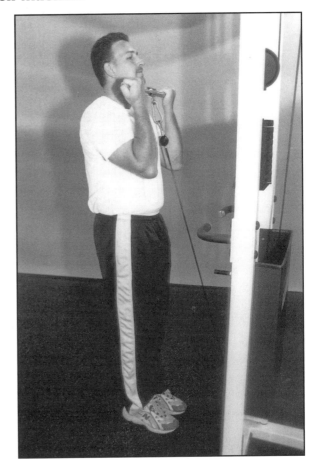

This benefits your biceps.

1. Stand erect with your feet together in front of a low pulley.

2. Grasp the short bar of the low cable with your palms up.

3. Stand back from the pulley to allow your arms to support your weight when extending your arms.

4. Curl the bar up in a semicircular motion until your forearms touch your biceps.

5. Keep your upper arms close to your sides.

6. Return to the start using the same path.

7. Exhale on the pull and inhale on the return.

Curl, Seated Alternating Dumbbell

This exercise develops, shapes, strengthens, and defines the whole biceps muscle and strengthens your forearms.

1. Hold a dumbbell in each hand.
2. Sit at the end of your bench (a chair will work, too) and place your feet firmly on the floor.
3. Keep your back straight and your head up.
4. Hang your arms downward at arms length with your palms facing inward.
5. Curl the dumbbell in your right hand with your palm in until you pass your thigh, then rotate your palm up for the remainder of the curl to the height of your shoulder. Flex your biceps muscle.
6. Keep your palm up while you lower the dumbbell until you pass your thigh, then rotate your palm inward.
7. Keep your elbows close to your sides. Keep your body steady. Only move your arms.
8. Do the repetition with your right arm, then repeat the curl with your left arm and so on, alternating sides for the number of reps indicated.
9. Exhale while you curl the dumbbell up, and inhale while you lower the weight down.

Note: This exercise also can be done standing erect with your feet wider than shoulder width apart. Alternatively, you may do this exercise on a bicep curl machine or with a floor pulley. It also may be done on an incline bench.

This exercise can be done in the last weeks of the conditioning phase and in parts four and five.

Curl, Seated Close Grip Concentration Barbell

This benefits your outer biceps.

1. Place the barbell on the floor near the end of your exercise bench.
2. Sit at the end of your exercise bench and place your feet greater than shoulder width apart.
3. Bend forward at your waist and grasp the barbell with both of your hands with your palms up at about six-to-eight inches apart.
4. Rest your elbows against your inner thighs about four inches up from your knees.
5. Curl the bar up until your forearms touch your biceps.
6. Lower the bar to its starting position while using the same path.
7. Exhale while you curl the barbell up, and inhale while you lower it down.

This exercise may be substituted for other biceps exercises in the conditioning phase and later.

Note: This exercise can be performed using either a close grip barbell or with an E-Z Curl Bar, holding the bar with both hands on the first curve of the bar with your palms facing upward. This version of the exercise can be done during the conditioning phase and later as an alternative to the other bicep exercises.

Curl, Seated Dumbbell

This develops, shapes, and defines the peak of the biceps and strengthens the forearms.

1. Hold a dumbbell in your right hand with your palm facing upward.
2. Sit at the end of your exercise bench (a chair will work, too) and place your feet greater than shoulder width apart.
3. Hold the dumbbell in front of you at arms length.
4. Bend slightly forward from your waist and place your left hand on your left knee. Keep your upper body down throughout the exercise.
5. Rest your upper right arm against your right inner thigh about four inches above your right knee.
6. Strongly flex your biceps. Curl the dumbbell up to shoulder height.
7. Maintain contact with your upper right arm to your right inner thigh all through the exercise.
8. Lower the dumbbell to the starting position by using the same path.
9. Exhale while you curl the dumbbell up, and inhale while you lower the weight down.
10. Once you have performed the necessary number of repetitions with your right arm, change the dumbbell to your left hand and repeat the exercise.

Note: You also can do this exercise in a standing bent-over position.

Preacher Curl

This benefits your biceps.

1. On a flat preacher bench, hold the dumbbell in your right hand, while the left acts as support, holding the edge of the pad.

2. Holding the dumbbell palm up, begin to curl the weight towards you, while keeping the arm next to the pad during the entire range of motion.

3. When you have completed the curl, and your forearm and biceps touch, lower the weight.

4. Repeat the movement while exhaling on the curl and inhaling on the return.

5. Do the number of repetitions with your right arm, then switch to your left arm for the necessary repetitions.

Note: This exercise also can be done dual arm with a curl bar.

EXERCISES FOR YOUR FOREARMS

Curl, Front Wrist

This benefits your forearms.

1. Sit at the edge of your exercise bench with a dumbbell in each hand.
2. With your elbows on your upper thigh, bring your wrist over your knees.
3. The exercise is based on the slight movement of the wrist, curling up, then returning to the starting position.
4. Pay attention to the integrity of the movement, making it smooth, slow, and careful.

Note: Do not snap your wrist.

5. You can practice this exercise with both hands simultaneously, or alternate left and right hands.

Curl, Reverse Grip Barbell

This benefits your outside forearms.

1. Stand upright. Place feet firmly on the ground, shoulder width apart.
2. Grasp the barbell with both hands about shoulder width apart with your palms facing downward (towards you).
3. Hold the barbell at arms length against your upper thighs.
4. Curl the barbell up until your forearms touch your biceps.
5. Keep your elbows as close to your sides as possible.
6. Lower the barbell to the starting position using the same path.
7. Do not swing your upper body or the barbell back and forth.
8. Exhale while you curl the barbell, and inhale while you lower it.

Note: This exercise may be performed with an E-Z Curl bar as well as with dumbbells.

Curl, Reverse Grip Wrist

This benefits your outside forearms.

1. Sit on the end of your exercise bench with your feet firmly on the floor greater than shoulder width apart.
2. Grasp the barbell with both hands.
3. Keep your palms up and your hands about shoulder width apart.
4. Lean forward and place your forearms on your upper thighs.
5. Put the backs of your wrists over your knees.
6. Lower the barbell downward as far as possible while still maintaining control of the bar.
7. Curl the barbell back up as far as possible.
8. Keep your forearms in place. Do not move them up and down your thighs.
9. Exhale while you raise the barbell up, and inhale while you lower it down.

Note: This exercise may be performed by using one or two dumbbells at a time or by curling the bar(s) over an exercise bench instead of your knees.

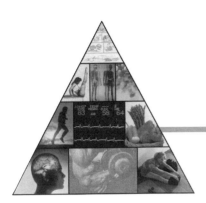

Glossary

abs: Abdominal muscles. A firm, muscular midsection not only looks great, but also helps to support your back. When your abs are extremely worked out and lean as a washboard, you get that "rippled" look.

aerobic: Describes exercises that require oxygen and involve movement of the large muscles in your body. Some aerobic exercises are running, rowing, and bicycling.

anaerobic: Describes exercises that cannot support the body's flow of oxygen. Weight training is one such exercise.

barbell: Long metal exercise bar, about five to seven feet in length, used in weight lifting. Weights (plates) may be added and secured to each side.

bench: Supportive, padded exercise equipment especially designed for weight lifting. Can be a flat, inline, or decline bench.

biceps: A flexor muscle of your upper arms, the place where you traditionally "make a muscle."

burn: A burning feeling in the muscle resulting from heavy-duty workouts, which is caused by a build-up of lactic acid.

cardiovascular training: Exercises designed to strengthen your heart and blood vessels.

circuit training: Full body workout that requires you to go from one "weight station" (exercise machine) to the next, usually without stopping.

delts (deltoids): The large triangular muscles in the shoulders. Think of the Greek letter delta, triangular in shape, and you will get an idea of what delts look like.

dumbbell: Short weight bar, with detachable plates at each end.

general readiness: This includes an individual's physiological mobilization efficiency, which translates to an individual's functional work capacity and recovery, an increased tolerance of fatigue, and an increased alertness. It also includes increased safety and physical performance.

glutes (gluteus maximus): Your rear end.

ham (hamstrings): Rear thigh.

lats (latissimus dorsi): Better known as your back.

lean body mass: Everything in the body except for fat. 50-60 percent of lean body mass is composed of water.

military press: Type of exercise in which the individual sits on an exercise bench and presses a barbell overhead.

muscle: Bands or bundles of fibrous tissue that produce movement or maintain body position.

obliques (external obliques): Muscles on either side of the abdomen. When you are out of shape, you might have heard these referred to as your "love-handles."

overload principle: Working a muscle through a greater than normal load to increase its capability.

pecs: Your chest.

pumped: The intense feeling of having worked your muscles to the max. Muscles are made larger by increase in bloody supply to the area.

quads (quadriceps): Large muscle forming the front of the thigh.

reps: Repetitions, the number of times you repeat an exericise in a set.

set: A fixed number of repetitions of an exercise.

specific readiness: This includes an individual's stamina, power to implement the use of force, the ability to stretch and use a full range of motion, and general movement.

strength: The ability of a muscle to produce a maximum amount of force.

strength training: Using resistance weight training to build maximum muscle strength.

traps (trapezius): The largest muscles in the back and neck.

triceps: The extensor muscle of the back of the upper arms.

universal machine: Weight training equipment where weights are on a track or rails, and are lifted by levers or pulleys.

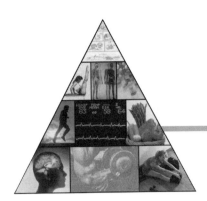

References

Alter, Michael J. 1998. *Sport Stretch: 311 Stretches for 41 Sports*. Champaign, Illinois: Human Kinetics.

American Dietetic Association. 2000. Position of the American Dietetic Association and the Canadian Dietetic Association: Nutrition for Physical Fitness and Athletic Performance for Adults. from: www.eatright.org/afitperform.html

American Heart Association. 2000. Dietary Guidelines for Healthy American Adults.

————. 2000. Target Heart Rates. www.americanheart.org

————. 2000. Women's Cardiovascular Disease Research and Prevention Act.

Griswold, Jon. 1998. *Basic Training: A Fundamental Guide to Fitness for Men*. New York: St. Martin's Press.

Hutchinson, Dennis. 2000. "Physical Fitness and Officer Safety." *Corrections Managers' Reports*. June/July.

Laliberte, Richard, Stephen C. George, and Editors of Men's Health Books. 1997. *The Men's Health Guide to Peak Conditioning*. Emmaus, Pennsylvania: Rodale Press.

Meja, Michael. 2000 "Ask the Experts: Ab Training." *Discount Nutrition*. April 24. www. discountnutrition.com

Moffat, Marilyn and Steve Vickery. 1999. *The American Physical Therapy Association Book of Body Maintenance and Repair*. New York: Henry Holt and Co.

O'Shea, Michael. 2000. "Parade's Guide to Better Fitness." *Parade Magazine*. June 18, page 19.

Parker, Robert B. and John R. Marsh. 1990. *Sports Illustrated, Training with Weights: The Athlete's Free-Weight Guide*. New York: Sports Illustrated Winner's Circle Books.

Pearl, Bill and Gary Moran. 1986. *Getting Stronger: Weight Training for Men and Women*. Bolinas, California: Shelter Publications, Inc.

Shangold, Mona and Gabe Mirkin. 1985. *The Complete Sports Medicine Book for Women*. New York: Simon and Schuster.

Smith, Michael E. 1990. "Michigan Officers Shape Up: Program Helps Officers Get Fit, Cut Stress." Corrections Today. July, page 176.

Stanford Center for Research in Disease Prevention and the Stanford Alumni Association. 1996. *Fresh Start: The Stanford Medical School Health and Fitness Program*. San Francisco, California: KQED Books.

U.S. Department of Agriculture. 2000. *Dietary Guidelines for Americans, 2000*. Washington, D.C.: Department of Agriculture.

U.S. Department of Health and Human Services. 1996. *Physical Activity and Health: A Report of the Surgeon General*. Atlanta, Georgia: Centers for Disease Control and Prevention.

Vedral, Joyce L. 1997. *Weight Training Made Easy: Transform Your Body in Four Simple Steps*. New York: Warner Books.

Voight, Karen. 1996. *Voight Precision Training for Body and Mind*. New York: Hyperion.

TRAINING LOG:

This page may be photocopied.

Day: _____ Start Time: _____

Date: _____ Finish Time: _____

Muscle Group	Exercise	Target Wt./Reps	Rest	Comments